HAUNTED *by* WORLD WAR II

Written by one of the last
East Prussians to settle
in the United States.

Herwig G. Schutzler

Lancaster, Pa./Lititz, Pa.

Preußen Memel Deutsches Land in fremder Hand Heydekrug

Haunted by World War II

by Herwig G. Schutzler

Library of Congress Number: 2020905195

International Standard Book Number: 978-1-60126-673-6

Masthof Press

219 Mill Road | Morgantown, PA 19543-9516

www.Masthof.com

Dedication

I am dedicating this writing to my grandchildren, listed here in order of their birth date:

Magdalena Grace Schutzler
Megan Elisabeth Schutzler
Erik Thomas Schutzler
Hannah Marie Schutzler

Map design by Andy Green, CA, Layout/Projection Data from "Natural Earth."

Laudschen
(born, 1936)
Copenhagen
Berlin
(Dash for freedom–1955)
GERMANY
Erfurt (1951–1955)
Frankfurt
(Land Survey Office, 1955–1956)
(Geodetic Institute, 1956–1960)

Table of Contents

Foreword

Most historical accounts, usually, start with a foreword. The pages that follow are describing the events in the life of one man, his family, friends, acquaintances and colleagues. Nothing is fiction, all events did happen in real life. But, on occasions, the author takes the liberty of expressing his personal views. After all, he has lived through quite a number of different political regimes, had faced numerous philosophical, ideological and physical hurdles and felt, as a free human being, that he can do just that. As an amateur historian, he had the chance to not only read about human history, but he also experienced it personally. The decades described in these pages cover the last half of the 20th century and the beginning of the 21st century. He created this as a looking glass for the following generations to focus on past events and, perhaps, find out why they happened.

Preface

I am as much a victim of the National Socialist Movement of Adolf Hitler as many other millions of German people or any other people. That movement had its rise right after World War I. The shortsighted victors of that war did not see what they had created with their harsh conditions against the loser of the war, Germany.

There are always victors and losers, not necessarily the right ones and the wrong ones. The social and economic conditions in the world in general at that time were feeding strong national feelings among nations, not just Germany. The Poles had suffered again under the Soviet and German dominances. The French were embarrassed. Czechoslovakia had been carved out of the Hapsburg Empire, two very different groups of people now one country. Other regions of that Hapsburg Empire were given to various countries as new territory, seeding mistrust and hate. Italy wanted to become a Roman Empire again. And England was in envy of the German industrialization and in fear of its military power.

Then came the economic breakdown of the 1930s. People started to look for help, in whatever way they could. Germany had always been a very strong military nation, with a strong will to dominate and secure itself. Hitler's political group saw its chance and grabbed it very quickly. The German population saw an end to their economic struggles, the industrialists saw great opportunities to make good profits, and various political groups within Germany pursued their own ideas. At least they tried, although they failed and so did the rest of Europe.

The rest is a history of which many smarter people then I have written plenty about. But I like to give credit to one person in Germany. His name is Guido Knopp. He is an honored German historian and one of the first to direct the world's attention to one of the barbaric results of Allied Agreements ending World War II and the subsequent destruction of Prussia totally and Germany almost totally. His book *Die Grosse Flucht, the Destiny of the Expelled* was published in 2001, describing in great detail the horrors of ordinary people fleeing from war and death, in the process losing all they ever possessed. My family and I were part of that human tragedy.

Allow me to introduce you to only one of many of those horrors, the sinking of the German ship *Wilhelm Gustloff* on January 30, 1945. This 2,000-passenger ship was loaded with 10,000 people, mostly civilian refugees, half of them children and wounded German soldiers. The ship was torpedoed by a Soviet submarine—a little over 1,000 souls were saved. The rest perished and are at the bottom of the Baltic Sea.

It is my fervent hope, that our grandchildren or their children will not have to ever experience something this traumatic. We here in the United States have the only hope in the world today to help to prevent another tragedy like this—no matter what all sorts of people are saying about the shortcomings of our political system. It is not the best mankind has come up with, but at the moment it is the only one trying to help oppressed people in the world by giving them hope, just as we were hanging on the forbidden radios in East Germany in the 1950s, listening to real news from the West. There are plenty people in the world today hoping to come here and live in real freedom.

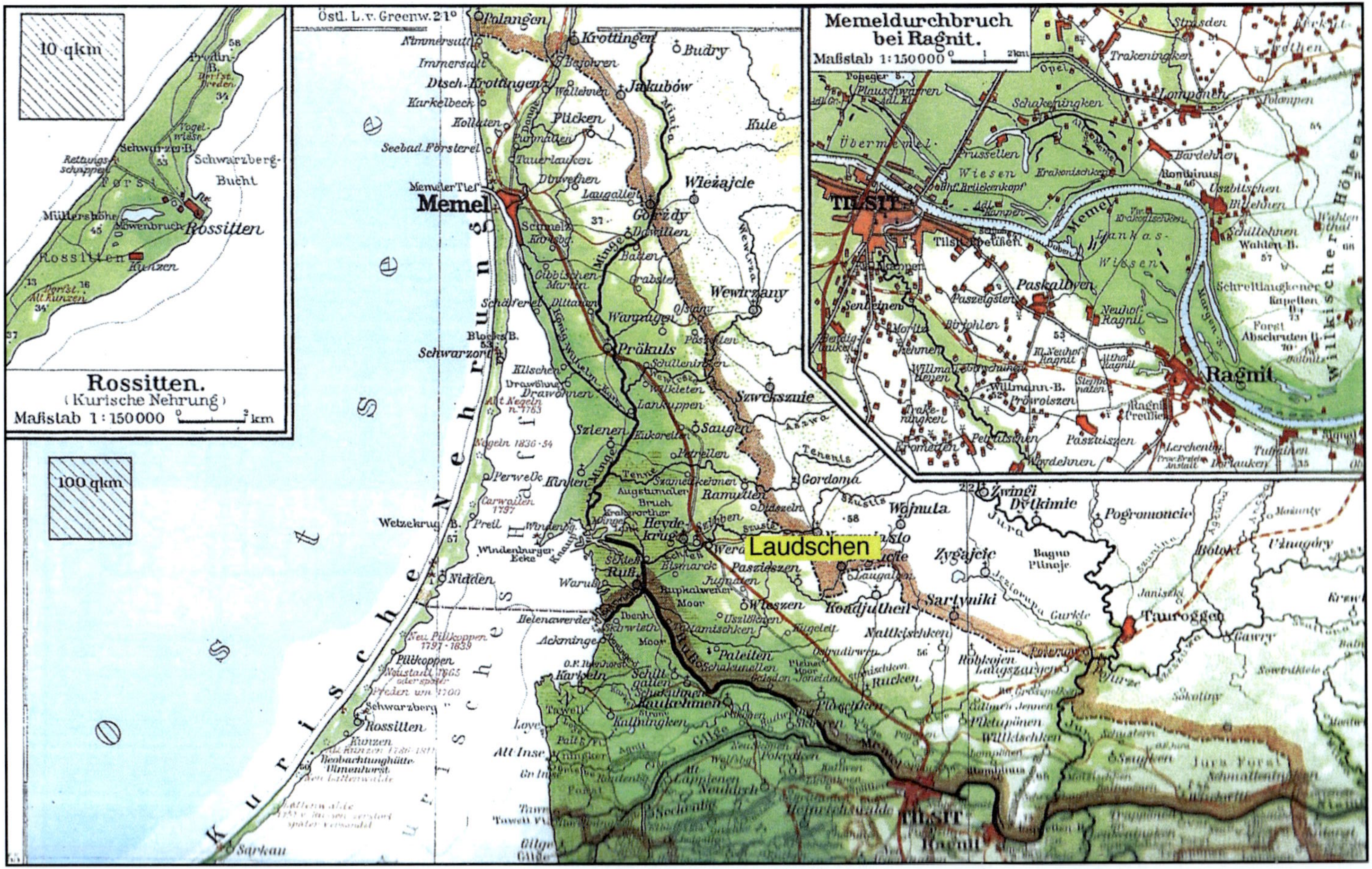

Memeldurchbruch bei Ragnit.
Maßstab 1:150000
Rossitten.
(Kurische Nehrung)
Maßstab 1:150000
10 qkm
100 qkm
Östl. L. v. Greenw. 21°
Memel
Tilsit
Ragnit
Laudschen
Heydekrug
Prökuls
Polangen
Krottingen
Tauroggen
Kurische Nehrung
Kurisches Haff
Ostsee
Rossitten
Nidden
Schwarzort

CHAPTER 1

Early Childhood

I was born on June 10, 1936, in Memelland, the German province of East Prussia, close to the border with Lithuania. At this time, Adolph Hitler was in complete control and had moved Germany toward being a military power in Europe. Germans in the frontier regions felt very patriotic and connected with the "Fatherland." It was good to be called a German.

I was the 3rd child of a rural schoolteacher and his wife who were living in the village of Laudschen. Laudschen is now called Lauciai, near the former Heydekrug, which is now called Silute in Lithuania. My father, Heinrich Eduard Schützler, was born in 1887 in Kairin. My father had searched his ancestry, a requirement by the 3rd Reich, back to 1784 in East Prussia and had told me that the Schützlers before had come from Swabia (Schwaben). They had been persecuted as Protestants by the

Left: Memelland, in the province of East Prussia, Germany, close to the border with Lithuania. Reprint of Weltbild Atlas 2009, *original work 1926* Heimatatlas für Ostpreussen. *My birthplace, Laudschen is highlighted in yellow.*

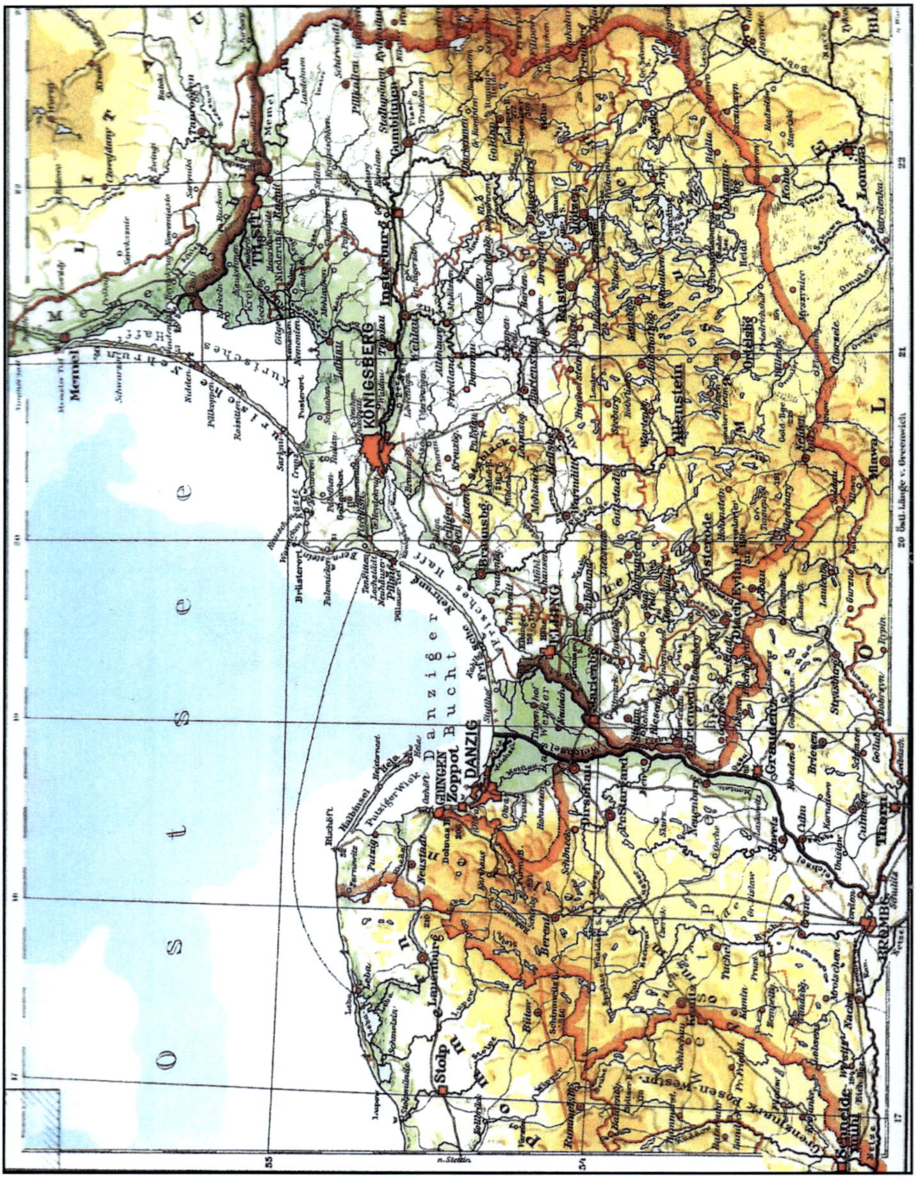

East Prussia (Ostpreussen) in 1926. Reprint of Weltbild Atlas 2009, *original work 1926* Heimatatlas für Ostpreussen.

ruling Catholic classes of the clergy and aristocracy and had gone to East Prussia by invitation of the Prussian ruler in order to have religious freedom. My father's younger brother had emigrated to Brazil, as had my paternal grandfather's younger brother done earlier. Today there are quite a few Schützlers living in Brazil in the State of Sao Paulo.

All the men on my father's side of the family had been teachers. The earliest one was a teacher and tailor at the same time. Picture this: He would have been sitting on a low table of considerable size, working on some piece of clothing, while his pupils would be sitting in front of him and he would direct them what to do. Tailors back then were measuring with a wooden tool called *Die Elle,* something similar to a yardstick. If a pupil required some reminder of discipline, the tailor/teacher would smack them with the stick, a very effective attention getter. My mother's family were fishermen and farmers for many generations. My mother, Maria Magdalena (Markscheit) Schützler, was born in Minge in 1908.

My parents were married December 4, 1927, in the St. Johannis Kirche in Memel. My siblings and I called our mother *Mutti*. My father was the schoolteacher for the rural region and during Hitler's rise became a believer in the new regime. As a result he ranked as an important person in the community, together with the mayor and the merchants. My siblings and I called him Papa. We resided in a building that was attached directly to the schoolhouse. This was the house in which I was born.

My sister Traute was born on August 28, 1928, in Paupelnpeter, Memelland, and my brother Wolfgang was born on

January 10, 1932, in Clauspuschen, Memelland. My father was moved around a lot as a German teacher by the different authorities, either Lithuanian or occupying Western forces after the Treaty of Versailles.

In the 2nd-floor attic a room was built as sleeping quarters for my sister Traute, my brother Wolfgang and myself. There was a dividing wall separating the boys from the girl. In age we were 4 years apart from each other; I being the youngest and my sister the oldest.

Downstairs were the eat-in kitchen, dining room, master bedroom and a large living room that also served as my father's study. In the study was a telephone that had a crank on the side. One lifted the receiver, cranked the handle a few times and the phone dispatcher would answer and then connect the call. Obviously there were very few phones in the area. Next to the living room/study was a large dining room. This room was not used very often—only on special occasions or when we had company for dinner. It was also the room where the Christmas Eve (*Heilig Abend*) family celebration would be held. A few days before *Heilig Abend* the room became off limits to me as the youngest of the family. The large dining room table had been decorated with the finest linen we had. I heard all sorts of commotion and as a small curious child became very excited. I knew *Knecht Ruprecht* (Santa Claus) would appear on *Heilig Abend* and we children would have to have either a poem or a Christmas song ready for *Knecht Ruprecht* to hear.

After supper, we all gathered in the study and our father would read the Christmas Story from Luke, using the Bible. Then our father would go into the basement to get some wine, making it appear as if he was busy and accounted for! Then we heard a small bell ring from the dining room, our mother would open the door and there was the Christmas tree in all its glory. Filled with ornaments and tinsel (made from lead!) and many real candles were flickering their golden lights. This was an awesome sight to behold. To this day I continue the tradition of real candles on a Christmas tree, as do my sons and their families.

I was speechless at the sight of this beauty. The tabletop was covered, showing some mysterious bulges under the covers. There was a knock on the outer door and in came *Knecht Ruprecht*. He carried a bag and a stick and he would ask each one of the children how we thought we had behaved throughout the past year and each one of us had to recite a poem or sing a song. The whole time he would gesture with the stick, striking fear in my little heart. Then he gave each of us a wrapped gift and then walked out of the room. After that, my dad (who had mysteriously reappeared!) would remove the covers from the table's secrets. There were wrapped presents and a large colorful Christmas plate called *der bunte Teller*, filled with cookies, candies and some fruits. Oh what joy!

There was a double door connecting the dining room with the schoolhouse part of the building. A wide corridor separated the two parts of the building. The schoolroom, very similar to an Amish one-room schoolhouse, was very spacious with large windows facing the west side and part of the schoolyard. Children in first through eighth grades would attend this school. This was mandatory for children. Sometimes people would go on to high school and after that either a college or university. Königsberg had the famous Kant University, known for its liberal arts school.

Our house was surrounded by plenty of garden spaces. In the front were grass, flowerbeds, ornamental bushes and trees on one side of the house, and toward the back were berry bushes such as gooseberry and currants and the vegetable garden. On the school side was the schoolyard bordered by a row of large linden trees. The whole complex was surrounded on three sides by farm fields and a few hundred feet toward the south side was a gentle bluff going down towards a small river. The river's name was Schusste. From this river we would often in the summertime carry water up to the garden to water the plants. We all had chores to do in the vegetable garden. My father would mix water and chicken droppings, as fertilizer for the tomato plants.

On the bluff here and on the opposite side were the ancient riverbanks of the Schusste. There were farm fields on our side, maintained by local farmers, planting wheat, rye and oats. I often watched a farmer plow the field with a horse-drawn hand plow, opening up the rich dark soil. During harvest time, I saw him sharpen the scythe with a sharpening stone, unto which he would spit and when satisfied with the sharpness of the blade, he would swing the scythe from left to right and one could hear a singing sound caused by the steel blade cutting through the grain stalks. He would take a break, sitting by the field side, unpacking some very dark bread, a piece of smoked bacon and a bottle of Rye Schnapps!

An unpaved road went from the house down to the valley, where a wooden bridge anchored on concrete slabs would go over the river. The road dipped down from the bridge toward the valley floor as it curved its way toward the schoolhouse, lined by a long row of willow trees and topped at the end by an oak tree. That low part was always flooded in the spring with the annual snowmelt. We all had to walk this way towards the main road for shopping or my sister on her way to the train in the morning going to the high school in Heydekrug. My Papa and a neighbor constructed a wooden plank walkway by nailing them directly onto the willow trees and also attaching a

Lutheran Church in Heydekrug

handhold. Sometimes this footbridge would be slightly washed over by the flooding waters. One day I was walking with my sister across this footbridge when I slipped and fell into the high water. Only the fast reaction of my sister jumping right after me saved my life. I was forever fearful for my life near water after that. The road ultimately would lead to the main road, the whole distance being about one mile.

On the main road was a rail stop for a train connecting all the farm communities with the county seat Heydekrug, which today is known as Silute. Also on that main road was a grocery store with an attached pub, and a little further on were the flour mill and little post office. These were the only buildings resembling a village. Both the mill and the grocery sold farm supplies.

This was not a settlement in the sense of a village. Since it was all agricultural, the people lived on their farms (*Güter*). Life was peaceful, and food was plentiful and wholesome. Not too far away were some woods, consisting primarily of pine trees but also some areas with deciduous trees. There we often went to pick mushrooms. Papa as a country teacher was very knowledgeable about these things. The mushrooms I recall to this day to be the best were *Steinpilz* (*boletus edulis*) and *Pfifferlinge* (*Chantrelle*).

In the summer we spent three weeks vacationing in the fishing village of Nidden (now Nida) right in the middle of the sand dunes separating the Baltic Sea from the Kurische Lagoon. There was always the sea breeze keeping the air a little fresher and we would get ice cream! Sliding down the sand dunes was a lot of fun. Incidentally, these are one of the larg-

Father Heinrich, Wolfgang, Herwig and Traute in Nidden in 1939.

In Nidden in 1993 with Cousin Gertrud and Heidi.

est sea sand dunes in the world, arching from the southern mainland northeast for approximately 85 miles toward Memel (Kleipeda). The area is now a protected natural preserve.

Back in Laudschen we would do our daily chores during the week and on Saturday we took the train to Heydekrug to

Traute, Herwig and Wolfgang in front of study.

Herwig in front of study windows, 1993.

Magdalena Schutzler, 1939

do some shopping, for things such as fabric our *Mutti* needed to sew, and crispy hard rolls and special sausages. We visited the barber for a haircut or go to the dentist or whatever the needs might be. My sister attended high school (*Herder Schule*) in Heydekrug, and took the train in the morning and evening.

Music was an important part of our family life. *Mutti* played the accordion and the lute, our father played the organ that we had and he also played the violin. My sister and brother played flute and my sister also played piano. I was still too young to have learned an instrument. There were many evenings where we all would sing, learning new songs all the time.

We had no electricity, so the lights at night and in the wintertime came from either petroleum lamps or kerosene lamps, similar to ordinary camping lamps we use today. One day I remember a great activity throughout the house. Wires were laid and some small electric lamps were installed! Where did the power come from? There was an array of automobile batteries behind my father's desk that was the power source.

The radio became an important part in the life of our family. We were living in the German frontier land and the radio served as a connection to the Reich. Across the courtyard of the house was a rather large barn, where we kept tools and

Herwig at rear of house, ca. 1942.

Herwig at rear of house in 1993. Notice same door and windows! Notice a line, either electric or an antenna, running into the house.

carts, etc. In that barn were also the chicken coop and a stable for a pig. We kept one pig for a year and in the fall the butcher would come and butcher the pig and neighbor ladies and men would come and help make sausages and meat cuts. Papa had a smoke room upstairs in the attic. Sides of bacon and sausages would hang there over smoke coming from wet sawdust. What a wonderful smell! My mother's older brother August, who was a fisherman and farmer, would show up once in a while by bicycle and bring us fresh fish, including live eel. I did not like that, but I liked smoked eel.

Next to the barn was the outhouse. That was ok in the summertime, but could be a problem in the wintertime. The climate in that region is dominated by the prevailing winds from Russia and winter would start early. It would start around mid to late October and last through April with very low temperatures, mostly under the freezing point, and lots of snow. Going to the outhouse was at times an ordeal. Our father felt sorry for us children and built us an enclosed seat with a pot under the seat. Our father dubbed it the "*Locophone.*"

The snow would stay through the winter and sledding was always fun, down the slope to the frozen river. My brother Wolfgang and some of his friends would build igloos, pouring water over the whole thing to make them frozen solid. One time they had built a smaller one, with a very small opening. When it was finished, they put a pot into it with a water and carbide mixture. Then they sealed the opening with ice. We all moved away, waiting for the carbide fumes to bust the whole thing up with a loud bang! Well, that was a lot of fun. Our parents never knew, or so we thought. In order to keep us warm, our mother had knitted woolen stockings for our legs, using raw wool she got from local people that were spinning them from their shorn sheep.

My parents gave parties in the house, with the closer or distant neighbors attending. Sometimes they all would sing songs, accompanied by my father playing the harmonium (a small parlor organ) and my mother playing the lute (*Laute* in German). Our mother also played the accordion.

Then one day our lives started to change. It started gradually at first. The schoolhouse and grounds were used to garrison a large contingent of army troops. They stayed with us for a few weeks. This was part of the build up for Hitler's Operation Barbarossa, the subsequent invasion of the Soviet Union. It was very exciting for us children to watch the daily activities of the troops. In the evening there would be soldiers standing guard duty. The troops left and we as kids forgot about the war.

Then came a very drastic life-changing event—our father was called up to serve in the army. He was 57 years old and was assigned to the southeastern front, ironically the same theater of war he had experienced for 4 years in WW I.

I remember my birthday 1944 very well. *Mutti* had arranged for a garden party for me; it was a very warm day and we had fun with some other children from the neighboring farms. One of the adults said, "Be silent for a minute and listen." We heard a continuous rumble and asked, "Is there a thunderstorm coming?" We were told, "No, what you hear is artillery exchanges from the Russian front back east." War had touched us at that moment directly and would not let go of us for the next 5 years! I never forgot that birthday for the rest of my life. Since my birthday is in June, it usually is very warm that day and therefore my mind will always take me back on my birthday for a fleeting moment to that day in 1944.

From now on we, the younger ones, noticed the changes around us. The adults and older children now talked about war and refugees. A plane had crashed not too far from our house and the older boys dismantled a machine gun from the plane and also took some ammunition and assembled that in "our" bunker. We had built a bunker into the slope side of the river I had mentioned earlier. It was very nicely built with wooden boards and planks to brace it. As the youngest member of our war group, it was my duty to guard the bunker. I was to announce if any adult was coming our way. One day the boys put a shell into the firing mechanism of the machine gun and then hit the bolt with a long-handled hammer. The result was a very loud "Kaboom" echoing over the river valley. Nobody seemed to find anything out of place. As my brother turned 12 years of age, he had joined the young Hitler Youth, called *Pimpfe*. He wore his uniform to the troop meetings with great pride.

Then came the next and final blow to our life in Laudschen. My mother was told to pack what she thought was important to us and only what we could hand carry. The next morning we were told to meet at the rail stop for the train that was to take us to Memel (Klaipeda). We were told that this was a precautionary move. As soon as the German army was victorious in driving back the Russians, we would be allowed to go back home. Well, this was the start of a one-year long trek going slowly west, covering roughly 1,000 miles.

CHAPTER 2

Expelled From Home

It was August 1944 and we left the house in the early hours before sunrise and walked toward the rail stop. *Mutti* and my sister were crying. The train took us to Heydekrug, where we changed onto another train that took us to Memel. In Memel we were then trucked to the harbor. There we saw thousands of people like us, carrying their belongings and waiting to be told what ship or boat to board. There was a very good looking ship that used to be a modern whale-processing vessel with the name of *Walter Rau* and we were told that we would be going on it. As the authorities admitted the people on board, they soon realized that the ship was quickly becoming filled and that there were still too many people to be taken care of. We did not make it onto the ship and it left shortly after that. We were put into the hold of a low-hulled cargo barge, three of those were then put in tow by a harbor tug and we moved out into the Baltic Sea that evening. Our destination was a harbor near Königsberg (now Kaliningrad).

Königsberg

It was windy and rainy that night. We were laying in the hold with hundreds of other people—old people lamenting, children crying—and I needed to use a bathroom. My sister took me on deck, which was slightly slanted from the center to the sides. They had an outhouse constructed on the top and we had to be very careful moving across the deck, as it was raining and the sea somewhat choppy.

That same night the Walter Rau *was attacked by British or Russian bombers and sank with the people on board. Fate had saved us from certain death.*

We arrived sometime the next day at a dock and boarded a train for Königsberg. Shortly thereafter we came to a refugee camp on the outskirts of the city. The following night the Allies staged an air raid on Königsberg, fire bombing that pretty well destroyed a good part of the city. To us as children it was a very spectacular event—seeing the crisscrossing searchlights of the air defense, hearing the staccato of the antiaircraft guns and also seeing target markings for the bombers. They hung in the sky glimmering and shaped like Christmas trees and that is what we called them.

Next we were moved again a little deeper into East Prussia, southwest of Königsberg. This time there was no camp. The people were distributed among small towns and villages. My family was housed in one of the houses of a local farmer and we stayed there for a while. We were waiting for the greatly expected announcement from the German Army, that they had defeated the feared Red Army and we all could go home. That announcement never came but what we got to see instead was a daily, steady flow of refugees moving by on the highway. It was mostly farmers with their belongings on top of horse-drawn wagons. Quite a few also had some livestock with them, primarily cattle. Sometimes they stopped for water, but most of the time they just moved on, trying to put some good distance between themselves and the Russians. These columns of people and their belongings were called *Trecks* in German. Finally in the early 2000s more and more of these events in words and pictures are being published in Germany.

We were afraid. What we feared were the Russians. This fear is what started to dominate our lives. We still had simple needs like eating, sleeping and keeping busy with life. But fear was always there. I learned very early in life what naked fear is and it would be with me for some time to come, well into the immediate years after the war.

The stories we started to hear from the other refugees were just awful. The Russians in their advancing conquest indiscriminately brutalized and killed anything that looked like or talked like a German. What these soldiers did to the civilian population was so horrendous and grotesque, that I will not write about it in detail here. They destroyed the homes and farms, raped and then killed the women and even girls, and shot the animals—leaving behind them a swath of total destruction. It was revenge, as urged on by the Soviet leadership. The Soviet commentator Ilja Ehrenburg was their mouthpiece.

On the farm where we were staying, in this advancing time of summer, we tried to be helpful by doing chores around the house and the fields. The German Army had launched a counteroffensive and my mother, together with some other people, went back to our home in order to get some more of our needed belongings and clothing. Winter would be with us and we needed protection from the elements. Two suitcases full of these things came back with my mother. It was also the last time she saw what used to be her house and whatever else remained behind that she could not bring with her.

The frontline started to move again, coming our way, and so we had to leave again. This time our hosts also had to leave with us. The continuous heartaches and losses to all these people as witnessed by me, being a child of 8 years, never really has left my memory to this day. It marked all of us psychologically for the rest of our lives. My mother's life was destroyed, her home gone. My sister until the day she died never wanted to talk about these events and never considered going back for a visit. My brother talked for many years about going back to "our" home, but when time came for a visit in 1993 he was too ill to travel.

From this point on it was a slow but steady trek, mostly by train through southern East Prussia going into Poland. We were in rail boxcars, on a bed of straw for soft bedding. The trains would go through empty villages and past abandoned farm animals in the fields. We heard the painful cry of dairy cattle that had not been milked. We saw columns of German Army units moving on the highways in the east and west direction, representing retiring and fresh troops. Some people would die, the old or the sick and then be buried along the rail line. Graves that are long forgotten contain the bodies of people that were now the only ones staying behind. My cousin Gertrud had a baby sister who died of starvation on their *Treck* from home. She was buried near Heiligenbeil, East Prussia (near the coast) and then the family moved on!

Low-flying aircraft attacked us, shooting their guns at the train. The train stopped, we all rushed out into some ditches until the planes left and then continued on with the journey. Sometimes our train would stop for hours in the middle of nowhere; sometimes we were on some side rail for days, probably because of either some war action or letting German Army troops take the main track. The first large town was Torn (now Torun) and than Posen (now Poznan). All the time the German Army tried to either halt or slow down the advance of the Red Army in order to give us refugees a chance to escape. The goal was to reach the advance of General Patton's American Army now moving toward the Elbe River. They moved very slowly and we never understood why, until years later when we all learned that all of that was nothing but political maneuvering among the four powers—all on the backs of millions of uprooted people. The stories of what the Russians were doing filled our ears and minds with naked terror.

The next point of destination for us, we were told, would be the province of Saxony. It was now winter. Food, water, warm clothing and sleeping were in short supply and it only grew worse. The one camp I remember was in some park, with some summer pavilions, some of these enclosed. There were bunk beds filling some rooms, but no mattresses and no heat or cooking facilities. We cooked outside on some mysterious German Army metal boxes, probably ammunitions boxes. The tops had been scraped clean with sand. We took trees down in the park for firewood and roasted either potatoes or roots.

We were moved again and came to a small village in Saxony with the name of Niederwürschnitz not too far from the city of Chemnitz. All of a sudden we were directly on the frontline between the American and German forces. For the next few months there was total war all around us. The defending German units belonged to the famous Waffen SS (gray uniformed fighting force, not to be mistaken for the deadly black uniformed political SS).

The war rolled over all of us back and forth. For some days the Germans held the village and for some days the Americans. The other side then bombarded with planes or with artillery. We were housed in pre-fabricated buildings, with thin walls sitting on gravel. The next air raid shelter was about 500 yards away, the basement of a movie theater. I remember being in that shelter for days at a time. No lights, just candles and no food. Food was whatever was available through the German Army. I remember to this day the taste of a root that normally was given as feed to horses, about 10" to 12" long and 2" in diameter. We ate it—either cooked, raw or roasted. Never did we see milk, meat, fat or any other food. Water was the only drink to be had. At one time we thought big changes in food were coming. We received rice and rice and again rice, cooked in water. Or we would walk over the harvested wheat and rye fields and look for husks containing the kernels. We would collect these, take them home, clean them out by getting rid of the chaff and then grind the kernels to get some sort of flour. Wow, different food! One night the city of Chemnitz was fire bombed and we saw the whole sky ablaze. It was awesome and eerie and ashes would rain over us.

Each day we observed huge formations of B-Bombers flying very high over us toward their targets. The whole air would vibrate from the sound of the combined engines and the sky glistened, reflecting the sunlight off the planes' bodies. They were most likely on their way to bomb the city of Berlin.

Sleeping had become a rare luxury for all of us. I would cry, when I would be awakened from my sleep to either go to the shelter or some other safe area. Sometimes we did not have enough warning to go to the shelter and the soldiers would be all around us fighting. We had to take all the mattresses, blankets and anything else to line the walls of one room, in order to shield us from flying bullets.

My brother was nearly 13 and as a member of the Hitler Youth he was called to help out as a First Aid assistant. One day he came into the house ashen-faced and sick to his stomach. A German Citizen-Soldier (*Volkssturm*) had fired an anti tank weapon by placing it against his shoulder like a rifle and it had torn off his arm. My brother had to administer medical help.

There was a paper mill nearby and one day it was bombed and for hours we were showered with ash and burned pieces of paper. There were daily bombings from aircraft or artillery bombardments and in between either tank battles or fiery infantry exchanges.

The fear for the life of her children must have been a terrible burden on our mother and all other women like her. There was no safety, very little or no food, and no clothing other than what we had with us. There was also no possible end in sight of this nightmare. These women were strong, as women usually are in similar circumstances. No wonder that many of them in later years would not be understood and supported by their children. And all of them maintained for the rest of their lives the tendency to hoard all things—might it be food or clothing or odd things such as light bulbs or buttons. We, the children of these mothers often do the same types of things as we watched our mothers do this and are looked upon by our children as being very strange!

This existence, our "world" within the context of war and what came after that had its own rules of morality and security. It was all about survival. That alone ruled the lives of the people. Once it was clear in the mind of all sensible people that Germany was losing the war, we all hoped for an end for many reasons. Mostly we wanted an end to the nightmare. On May 8, 1945, the news came that Germany had surrendered. We were all so elated when we saw the American tanks and troops roll through our town. My birthday was a few weeks later and my brother had saved a piece of chocolate he had gotten from a GI to give to me as a gift, what a treat! The Americans were going east we were told, to meet with the Russian Army at the Elbe River. It seemed to us that we were saved by the Americans from the wrath of the Red Army. We were wrong! Some weeks later all of the Americans moved back west and rumors started—the dreaded Red Army was coming!

The whereabouts of our father, who had been drafted, remained a mystery. We had not heard from our father until one day he stood on our door almost unrecognizable. He had a beard, tattered clothing and was thin as a rail. He had been a

POW in a camp run by the Czech Army in the town of Graz, Austria. He managed to escape from it and had walked approximately 360 miles to meet up with us. The joy was short-lived for us children. Our parents had decided to separate! Not great timing. I guess life goes on, no matter what the circumstances might be. After all we are all people with our own ideas and tolerances. This breakup was obviously discussed many times between us children and somewhat less with our parents; only to realize, that these two people had to do what they thought was best for them. They both did everything to promote good contact between us children and our father or mother. Some of us made our own choices over the years. As for me, I spent all my summer vacations with my father and look back on these visits with a happy smile on my face.

I want to mention an ugly practice of war, the rape of women. Whenever groups of refugees were caught by advancing Russian troops there were rape stories. As a nine year old I understood the meaning and process of rape and it horrified me. Rape is a brutal and feared act that every woman dreads. These rapes left a stigma on families back then. My brother and I were constantly in fear for our mother and sister. The fear for this dreaded "war practice" was constantly hanging over all of us, with gang rape being the most feared. It was hard for me to hear about it then and I find it still extremely hard to hear about it now. We were told that this is what Slavic conquerors do, especially the Asians. I guess it depends on the time of history and who the conqueror is and who the conquered are. German people were not valued very highly at that time as a result of what the German Armies had been doing in the previous years. But as always, it is the civilian population that does all the suffering.

It was years later that we realized that we had become part of the largest, forced removal of a native and permanent population of a sovereign nation in the history of mankind. About 15 million Germans would be removed from East Prussia, Silesia and the Sudetenland. It is estimated that about 2 million people died during these "removals." This horrible nightmare inflicted upon a people has not been dealt with in any history book that I am aware of. It is not being taught in schools and as a matter of fact, it is being avoided in any political discussion in any forum. It was a travesty committed by the victors of World War II. We were the victims.

There are private organizations today in Germany, consisting of former refugees from all these now occupied parts of Germany. These organizations are attempting to enlighten the world on what happened. They are *not* calling for the return of these lands; that would be pointless now. But they want the world to know about the truth of these forced removals. The German nation had to learn about the crimes that Hitler had done to other nations. The other nations should also know about the events that had followed the war and the subsequent horrific treatment of the German civilian population by the Red Army, as they thought they were justified in doing, since it had been ok'd by agreements among the Allies.

All of these tragic events were on the heels of what had been done to the German people and their land after the Treaty of Versailles. That alone was a hateful course of actions of the "victors" of the First World War. The Second World War saw a total disregard for the human rights, dignity and lives of the people in East Prussia, West Prussia and Austria. Josef Stalin, with a total approval from the Western Allies, forcefully removed all the German people. This way not another plebiscite, like in 1926, could be done there! And nobody in today's political and philosophical world is talking about these events.

I ask all of my relatives and friends to preserve all my writings and collections of historical material collected over the years. This includes the stories I have shared with you, so that this never gets lost or forgotten. Only then can we learn from and perhaps not repeat this tragedy.

I have always had one critical question left unanswered. Why would the people of East Prussia or Silesia have to give up their legitimate lands, homes, possessions and often their lives for the crimes of Hitler? These were their lands for hundreds of years, no matter what the Poles or the Lithuanians or the Russians have to say and are saying. I wonder why the people of Palestine have a right to land and a country? Why not the Germans?

Perhaps I do answer my own question this way. Over the past centuries, the Prussians and the Germans had embarrassed the Russians quite a lot. The Prussian kings and the German Field Marshall Hindenburg come to mind. Whenever the Russians tried to stop them, they failed. Then came Hitler's failures in Russia and the Western material support with the Lend Lease Act. Stalin saw the chance to avenge these previous Russians failures. He acted forcefully on the military front and on the diplomatic front. His goal was to destroy Prussia/Germany forever. He almost succeeded, finally occupying the entire German eastern lands. And with the approval of the Western Allies, Russia received East Prussia as a victor's price. In addition, he kept the Polish lands he had conquered and in turn gave the Poles the eastern portion of former German territories. What travesties as seen in the light of world events in this century.

CHAPTER 3

Trying to Settle in After the War

After the war, my family was moved a little further west to the town of Mühlhausen in Thuringia. There we moved into two rooms of a house owned by an old spinster lady. We were allowed to use her kitchen and bathroom. We boys slept in one room and our mother slept with our sister in the other room. A new life would start now.

As we all had feared and dreaded, the Soviet Red Army was now moving in. Life in this part of Germany would forever change. Our town received a garrison of Red Army troops and they were housed in the former German Army barracks. At first we saw very little of them. At night the officers marched them out in company strengths and in formation and they marched them through the town singing. Perhaps to give them fresh air but most likely to put some fear into our hearts and also let us not forget, that we were now occupied.

All over the Soviet Zone, the Russians started to dismantle anything of industrial value that had survived the war. In our town was an electric power plant, fired by burning coke. That plant had three turbines; two of these were taken apart, boxed in huge shipping containers and then put on a train destined for Russia. The same thing was done to railroad tracks. Entire rail yards were stripped to the bare minimum of operation. Tracks connecting two stations and having more than one pair of tracks would be cut down to one track. War reparation! As the Marshall Plan started to help rebuild Western Europe, the Russians destroyed what was left over from the destruction of the war. Again, these things are never mentioned in any history book, in the U.S. or in Germany to this day.

The make-up of the Russian garrison was changed. Fresh troops were brought in, replacing the combat troops. These new troops were made up of mostly Asian people. They had very little knowledge of Western life, customs and comforts, but they now wanted all of that for themselves. Flushing toilets were looked at in wonderment and watches became their targets to take away from people. It was not unusual to see a soldier wearing 2-3 watches. Of course we also heard the not-so-funny stories of Russian soldiers throwing a watch away after it had stopped ticking, thinking it was defective, not knowing it needed to be wound up again.

There were now constant raids on German homes and apartments, including our own. In the middle of the night there would be a commotion on the street and we looked out of the window and watched. There would be two to three Russian soldiers with an officer. They demanded entry into a building and then systematically search all rooms. In the days close after the war's end, they would shout, "Where is Hitler?" They would rummage through people's belongings and if they saw something to their liking, they took it. This practice of stealing was stopped somewhat early in 1946.

At first there was nothing to be bought. No stores were open—they had nothing to offer. There was no food to be bought. Like we did during the war, we would go out to the harvested farm fields and look for left over potatoes in the soil or we would go over the wheat or rye fields and look for broken off sheaves and collect these. At home we would dig the grain out of the sheaf, grind them up and have some great food to eat. The authorities set up open public soup distribution centers. They were German Army field kitchen units and once a day we would stand in line and wait to be issued a container full of some watery "vegetable" soup. This went on for some time.

Then some real food appeared. The bakers, for example, would be issued flour to bake bread. A public announcement was made that bread would be available and of course we had to have food stamps for that. They announced, for example, that the bread would be available at 9 a.m. Tuesday. Queue lines started to form before dawn and we would do that in shifts, either my sister, brother, mother or I. I hated this duty. There always were bullies who pushed their way ahead, especially ahead of small children. The weather could be bad and after standing in line for hours it would be announced that no more bread was available for the day and we would go home empty-handed.

When we were fortunate enough to get some bread our mother locked the bought loaf in a cloth wardrobe, the only thing she had available with a key, so that we would not sneak an extra slice. It had to last for some days for the three of us. I remember standing in front of that wardrobe and sniffing at the crack of the door, oh how delicious the smell was! I still think of it today, every time I smell fresh bread. The butcher would get meat and the same process repeated as with the bakery. The butcher took any and all meat or bone scraps and boiled it, added salt to it and then announced, "Buy some broth!" Back in line we would go to get some of that fantastic stuff.

After one year of no school, they reopened and some sort of normalcy appeared. We had to bring a bowl with us in the morning, so that we could receive our lunch. That consisted mostly of some soup or porridge. I only had one pair of shoes and one day, on my way to school, one sole came halfway off. All day I walked around throwing my foot sort of in front, so that I might not stumble. My brother had gotten a cobbler's tripod, tacks and a hammer, and a strong needle and some thread and he would repair our shoes. My mother got a job as a seamstress in a textile factory making clothing.

Close to the building we called home was a small distillery and Russian GI's would stop us in the street and ask where the "*Schnapps fabrika*" was. We said, "Give us some *Machorka* and we will tell you." They would reach into a pocket of their uniform pants and pull out a handful of *Machorka*. This was a Russian Army issue of very coarse tobacco, made mostly from tobacco leaf stems.

We in turn sold this tobacco to the smokers among the German population. Any form of tobacco became very strong currency. My brother became quite an expert merchant. We would hear that somewhere on the Baltic coast herring was available. But it had to be bartered in exchange for an item they up north did not have access to. This could be tobacco, uncut leather or building nails. My mother would come back with the fish and sell it to other people. My mother had some valuables such as jewelry or a camera. She traded those items with the local farmers for food for us. Boy would they take advantage of this situation. But oh well, we survived.

In the winter of 1946-47 I broke my left femur in a luge accident, smashing right into a tree and breaking the bone into small pieces. My brother and his friends tied me to the sled and pulled me home and carried me with the sled up into the apartment. I had so much pain that they could not get me off the sled. The clothing was cut off and we saw my broken and very swollen leg now shorter than the other one. An ambulance got me to the hospital and it was determined that I needed an operation in order for the surgeon to go in and try to repair the bone. At first they ran a steel bar though the leg, right over the knee joint and fastened this to a wire that ran over a wheel at the foot of the bed and on that end they hung a weight. This was done in order to start pulling that leg back to its proper length. The weights were increased every so often. Then they cut the thigh open and wired the bone pieces together. Now the whole leg was put into a cast, stretching from my groin all the way to the toe joint. I was supposed to be able to wiggle my toes to keep them limber. After about a week they cut a window into the cast to get to the wound on top of my thigh in order to remove the stitches. Well, what presented itself was a very infected incision.

The wound was now treated every day with a solution that was to control the bacteria. Antibiotics were not yet readily available and so my body had to heal by itself. The cast was removed after about six weeks and my knee was now "frozen" as far as movement was concerned. Therapy started with heat treatments and then massage and then bending of the joint! I went through some very painful weeks of daily "forced" bending of the knee. I screamed so loud that the masseur had me moved into the basement of the hospital so that people would not hear my screaming. My mother tried to interfere, saying the masseur was too brutal but she did not get very far with that. Luckily for me, the hospital started to overflow with more sick people and after 11 weeks, I was discharged into the care of a town physician and another masseur.

The wound was still open and needed daily treatment. At first either my brother or my sister would carry me to the doctor's office and to the massage. Even though I was ten years old I did not weigh much. I started to learn how to walk, using a stick my brother fashioned for me, and then was able to walk on my own. After a while all was well and two years later I won the school championship in 5,000- and 10,000-meter runs!

A few years later my body was rejecting the foreign object wire, which started to become entangled in my thigh muscle. Another operation was needed to remove the wire. The wire is still in my possession today.

We lived in the town of Mühlhausen. Mühlhausen is a very old German city that was founded in 775 AD by Charlemagne and at the time we lived there had an approximate population of 50,000. The surrounding countryside is a rich agricultural region, with smooth rolling pastures and grain fields. The old medieval walls and towers and churches are still there today. It is an historic town of Germany and well worth a visit. The wall ran by the backyard of the building we lived in and we smaller children used it as a real prop for our games. There was still the now empty moat in front of the wall, giving our fantasy plenty of opportunities. Here in Mühlhausen, I had one more near drowning incident. Outside of town was a small lake and on one side a bathing area was roped off for the public to use. We went there quite often in the summertime. My brother and his friends were having fun in the water, as I was playing on the edge. Well, I must have tripped and fell in. Luckily, my brother saw that and pulled me out! This led to my fear of open water for the next few decades!

Not too far from our building was a rather large gothic church, with two massive towers. The whole building was constructed using locally quarried limestone. The name of the church is St. Divi Blasii and it had for a long time a very well known choir called the Bach Choir. J. S. Bach was organist in that church in 1707/8 and the organ that he played on was still in use at that time. My mother had enrolled me there for lessons of the Lutheran catechism in preparation for my confirmation. My voice was a very high "Boy-Soprano" and I was asked to become a member of the children part of the choir. When my voice changed later, I became a member of the baritone section of the Bach Choir and thought I had accomplished something very important. I was confirmed in this church.

Life started to get more normal now in this part of Germany, which would become part of the infamous German

Democratic Republic. The Russians formed a German police force, clad in dark blue uniforms and at first without weapons, just riot sticks. But soon they were issued small handguns and then followed by rifles. Heating, electricity and cooking gas was available only in limited amounts. The regular population would be told at what hours gas for cooking and electricity for light would be available. The industries had to run their machinery and also needed energy. So candlelight and perhaps petroleum lamps, if available, had to substitute a lot. Our first radio was a wonderful luxury and when electricity was available, added great entertainment to our home.

St. Divi Blasii in Mühlhausen/Thüringen

My brother organized night visits to the local industrial area at the train station in order to steal coal for our wood and coal fired heating stove. They took me along to stand guard over a hand drawn cart, while he and his buddies climbed over a fence. I remember being petrified to my bones thinking of things such as a shooting policeman or worse, being surprised by Russian soldiers. The local parks and small forests would soon be stripped of their trees. All of this took place in the late 1940s.

The communist propaganda started to be noticed by all of us. There were banners on the official buildings, and talk on the radio and in our schools about the wonderful relationship we as Germans were now enjoying with the peoples of the "glorious and victorious" Soviet Union. They had "delivered" us from the dread of the Nazis. We had to be "thankful" for the great "humanitarian act," costing them millions of lives. They were supposedly our friends and the people of the only free nation on earth and we must be friends forever.

CHAPTER 4

Schooling & Training, Life in the DDR (1953-1955)

We still had only the bare necessities of life available at that time and we sang sarcastically to the tune of the old National Anthem, "*Deutschland, Deutschland über alles,*" "*Deutschland, Deutschland ohne alles, ohne Butter, Brot und Speck und den Rest der Marmelade fressen uns die Russen weg.*" (Germany, Germany without anything, no Butter, Bread or Bacon and the little Marmelade there was, was eaten away by the Russians!) Of course this kind of thing bordered on dissent and would soon be considered an act against the state.

I was now in eighth grade and all our thoughts revolved around high school. Well, my dreams were dashed very fast. I was told that I was ineligible for high school, since high school attendance was reserved for children of workers and farmers, this being a state of workers and farmers. My father was a teacher, and worse still, he was a teacher during the Hitler regime! No matter that he had been through a "de-nazification process" conducted by the communist authorities. Since I had very good grades in the science subjects such as Physics, Chemistry, Biology and Geography it was suggested at a conference with my mother and I, that I should become a shepherd! Good grief! I had thought to go to high school and then enter the field of cinematography, because that is what I wanted to study.

My mother contacted my father, who incidentally was teaching again, and asked if he could help in my plight. Well, he wrote a letter to the school and it did something. I was now offered to attend a school in the town of Erfurt and study to become a cartographer. That would also require me to attend a practicum at the Justus Perthes Cartographic Institut in Gotha. Prior to this, I had to take another practicum at a local printing company, the reason for that requirement I never figured out.

At the tender age of 15 I learned how to draw lines and letters on lithographic stones and learn all about the printing process called lithographic printing. The state-owned company was called *The Thomas Müntzer Druckerei* and specialized in printing beautiful looking labels for liquor bottles. Thomas Müntzer was a contemporary of Martin Luther, fighting on the side of poor rural people against the feudal lords, therefore a hero in the eyes of the communist government.

After a few months I packed my belongings, moved to the town of Gotha and rented a small room containing a bed, a wardrobe, a chair (a stool, actually) and a washstand. There was no heat. The lady renting the room to me allowed me to do my homework in her kitchen in the evening, so that I had some comfort and also a table to write on. I would take the early train, around 6 a.m., to Erfurt in order to be there in time at 7 a.m. for classes at the school. Most of the time the train arrived fully packed with people. The only space I got was outside the compartments and I would be standing there, still sleeping a bit. We had classes every day, but some days I had to attend practical drawing lessons at the Institute in Gotha. So it would mean mornings in Erfurt and afternoons in Gotha on some days of the week.

My class consisted of 16 girls and 4 boys. Four male adolescents in a class with 16 girls! The very "wise" communist educators running the schools in East Germany had considered cartography a female profession and allowed some token males to take part. Well, good for us young guys. Not too bad we thought, but it also added some mental burden on us—complications associated with male and female relationships that we only understood in later years. Our studies consisted of German language, Russian language, Mathematics, Algebra, Geometry, Physics, Chemistry, Biology, Geography and Geomorphology, Cartography and of course Political Science.

"The historic struggle of the working masses of the world against their barbaric and cold capitalistic masters" was explained to us in minute detail. Any lingering thoughts in our minds that individualism and longing of personal achievement would be a normal human behavior, was to be forever eradicated. The masses rule now, so they said. Only the united working people under the leadership of the great Soviet Union can bring peace and prosperity to mankind.

One morning our political instructor, Herr Krug, walked into our classroom and announced with a broken voice and tears in his eyes that as he put it "the great leader of the Free Socialistic Peoples of the world, Joseph Stalin has died." We were stunned, what was to happen next? This world was without its *greatest visionary*, what was to happen to all of us? We were told to have no fear, that the great Soviet Union is blessed with having new leaders that will help and lead the poor and helpless masses. That sounds to me like the slogans of a certain political party in the U.S.A. in the 1970s to the present day. In all schools and factories a Stalin corner was now installed. It was a small table covered with a red cloth with his picture and some printed material of his utterances. We appropriately called it "The Altar." I can't help but think of the silliness of this today. What a blessing! We were saved again from being perhaps swallowed by some capitalist lurking in the dark. Think about this absurdity. German people were told by German people to admire Stalin! That man was one of the most brutal monsters ever to lead a country. Under his rule, countless people were killed. The numbers range from 10 million to 30 million! And people today still admire Communism? Why is that? Because the facts surrounding the founding of the Soviet Union and its subsequent conquests are not being taught in the schools.

And the media is full of Hitler's murders of people. Oh no, I am not belittling what Hitler did to his people and countless others. See my opening statement of these memoirs. I am saying fascism is a curse and had put the world into chaos and death. Communism, borne out of socialism, is much worse and very sadly, is still promoted and admired.

We were young and wanted some fun and so we went out and did! We organized a small music group and started to play at school and company dances. I had taught myself to play the accordion. We played a very mild, soft form of early rock—not to upset the ever present, checking party snoop. Around this time my brother had started to become very interested seeing what I was studying. He was a cabinetmaker by trade and applied at the Institute as a student and was accepted in a training program. He played the guitar and joined our band.

I eventually moved to Erfurt and again rented a small room containing the bare necessities and no heat, from an old couple. They allowed me to use their heated living room to do my ever-increasing homework. The Communist Party had organized "political house cells" and once a week those of us living in the apartment building would have to attend "study meetings." These were designed to "teach" us about all the wonderful things that would change in the world as communism prevailed. They promised a world with prosperity and peace, as mankind had never experienced before. *"Under the victorious leadership of the unfailing Soviet Union, we will crush the ugly capitalism forever and very soon."* Sometimes I had to bring an excuse card from the school to the cell leader if I had a school function and could not be there. The party needed to know at all times where everybody was.

My study and workplace in Erfurt was called *Vermessungsdienst,* belonging to the Inner Ministerium and we were issued the necessary documents that we had to carry with us at all times when in public.

There were banners on all public buildings proclaiming the great achievements done by the working class of the world, always under the leadership of the unfailing party in the *glori-*

Unterschrift des Ausweisinhabers
Schützler, Herwig
Name | Vorname
10.6.1936 | IX 0640692
Geburtsdatum | PA-Nr.
Kartenzeichner-Lehrling
Dienstbezeichnung
Erfurt, 26.1.55
Ausstellungsort und Datum
Unterschrift und Dienststellung
Kaderleiter

Dienstausw.-Nr. 360
Geltungsbereich: Vermessungsdienst Thüringen Erfurt, Anger 6 Tel. 5508
Gültig bis:

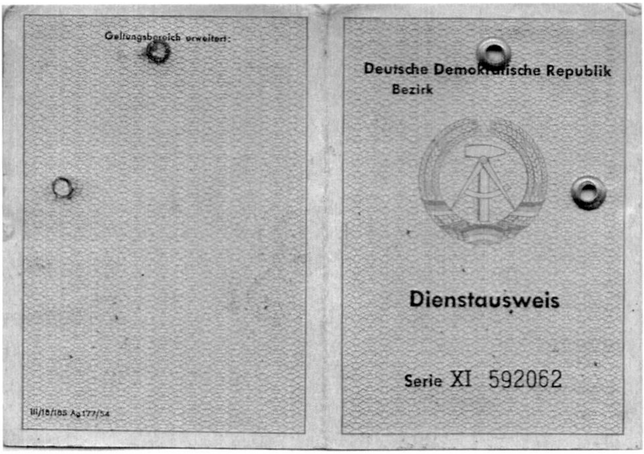
Geltungsbereich erweitert:
III/18/185 Ag177/54

Deutsche Demokratische Republik
Bezirk
Dienstausweis
Serie XI 592062

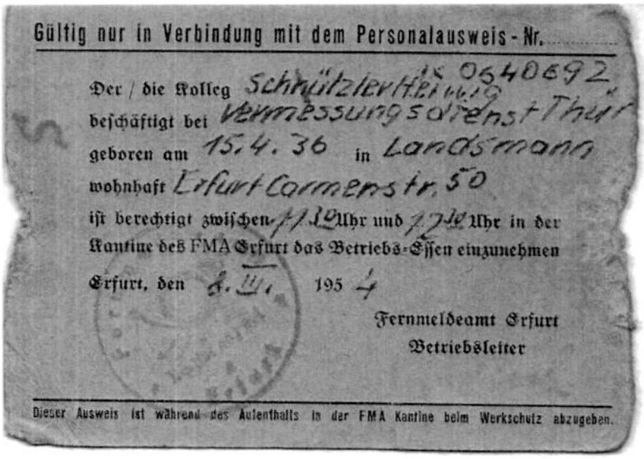
Gültig nur in Verbindung mit dem Personalausweis-Nr. IX 0640692
Der / die Kolleg Schmützler Heiwig
beschäftigt bei Vermessungsdienst Thür
geboren am 15.4.36 in Landsmann
wohnhaft Erfurt Carmenstr. 50
ist berechtigt zwischen 11 30 Uhr und 12 30 Uhr in der Kantine des FMA Erfurt das Betriebs-Essen einzunehmen
Erfurt, den 8. III. 1954
Fernmeldeamt Erfurt
Betriebsleiter
Dieser Ausweis ist während des Aufenthalts in der FMA Kantine beim Werkschutz abzugeben.

Top: In addition, we were issued a permit to be able to enter the Inner Ministerium.

Left: They had my birth date wrong and misspelled my birthplace!

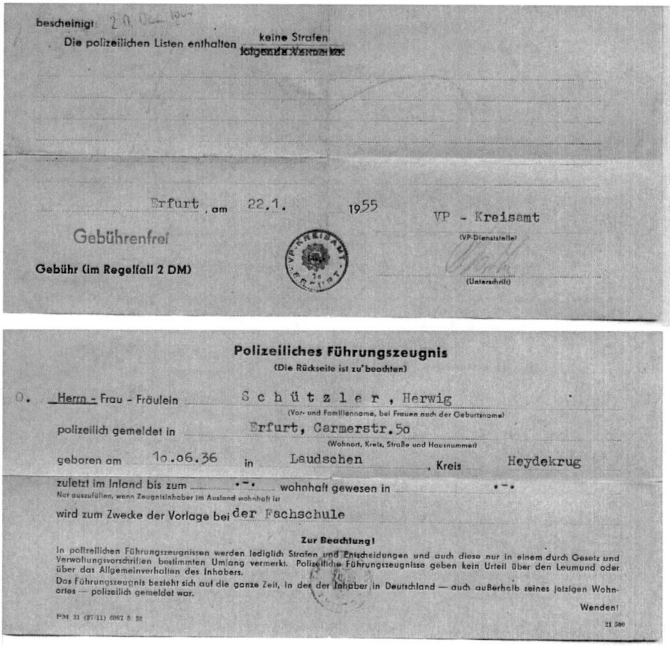

bescheinigt:
Die polizeilichen Listen enthalten keine Strafen

Erfurt, am 22.1. 1955

VP - Kreisamt
(VP-Dienststelle)
(Unterschrift)

Gebührenfrei
Gebühr (im Regelfall 2 DM)

Polizeiliches Führungszeugnis
(Die Rückseite ist zu beachten)

Herrn - Frau - Fräulein Schützler, Herwig
(Vor- und Familienname, bei Frauen auch der Geburtsname)
polizeilich gemeldet in Erfurt, Carmerstr.50
(Wohnort, Kreis, Straße und Hausnummer)
geboren am 10.06.36 in Laudschen, Kreis Heydekrug
zuletzt im Inland bis zum .-. wohnhaft gewesen in .-.
Nur auszufüllen, wenn Zeugnisinhaber im Ausland wohnhaft ist
wird zum Zwecke der Vorlage bei der Fachschule

Zur Beachtung!
In polizeilichen Führungszeugnissen werden lediglich Strafen und Entscheidungen und auch diese nur in einem durch Gesetz und Verwaltungsvorschriften bestimmten Umfang vermerkt. Polizeiliche Führungszeugnisse geben kein Urteil über den Leumund oder über das Allgemeinverhalten des Inhabers.
Das Führungszeugnis bezieht sich auf die ganze Zeit, in der der Inhaber in Deutschland — auch außerhalb seines jetzigen Wohnortes — polizeilich gemeldet war.

Wenden!

My background had been checked and authenticated by the police.

ous Soviet Union. Tell somebody often enough that he is stupid and after a while he will for sure believe it. We were told that the great scientists of Russia and the Soviet Union had come up with most of the results of scientific research and most of the inventions. Might it be television, radio, biological research, agricultural research, music and of course the understanding of the human mind. We quoted a poem, "*Russen schufen diese Erde, Sonne, Mond und Sternenheere, selbst der Adam und Gemahlin, stammen ab vom grossen Stalin!*" (Russians created the Earth, the Sun, the Moon and the Stars, even Adam and his wife were direct descendants of the great Stalin.) We always had to be careful and watch who would be around us and hear what we would be saying.

One of us four guys was such a person. He always let the teachers know how great he thought the socialistic system was. He would volunteer for any political activity and said out loud that he would report any anti-government remarks from anybody, even if it came from his own family. His father had been thrown into the Buchenwald concentration camp as a staunch member of the socialist party, who was in opposition to the now powerful communist ruling party. His father died shortly after having been released from Buchenwald and we always wondered who had tipped off the authorities about his political thinking. Incidentally, for years Buchenwald was kept open by the Soviets and used as a prison to lock up all those people who spoke out against communist rule. There were plenty of people doing just that. The Germans had just come out of Hitler's totalitarian nightmare. The same people that had been against Hitler and had been in jail, or worse, were now being thrown back into prison because they saw another menace to human, democratic thinking raising its head.

After that, the communists prepared the former concentration camp Buchenwald to be a memorial to the Hitler terror against the Jews. We, as members of the youth groups of the system, were herded through the camp. We saw first hand the rows of crematory ovens and the gas champers, resembling large shower rooms. We were taken to the mass graves and then had hours of displays of pictures and political instructions. This happened to me twice and it engraved a deep impression into my soul. It is amazing what a civilized people like the Germans would let happen! Well, the Hitler party had promised the German nation a return to its former glory and primarily promised the people a sound economy. They promised an economy that would bring plenty of jobs and good food on the table. The people believed that and followed. Things like that can happen here in the U.S.A., too. Promise the masses a lot, show them some success and off you go.

I spent some of my summer vacations with my father. He was teaching in Zethlingen, a village in the Altmark Region in NW East Germany not too far from Kalbe/Milde, where he later retired to and now lays buried there. On Sundays he would play the organ in the church. That organ was an old instrument with bellows that had to be worked by hand. I would do that, as my father played. He looked around the corner of the keyboard and nod to me, so I would know when to work the bellows. He had married again. His wife's name was Marie Kupries and she was born in Memelland. She really was a good wife to him. He had a little dog and the three of us would go for walks and he would tell me about his thoughts on life and his Christian beliefs. He said one will find God anywhere in nature. A person that goes to church every Sunday and prays and then lives a godless life during the week is not a Christian. He told me to be a good person, no matter what. He was also very sad that my sister Traute did not care for him and that my brother Wolfgang started to withdraw. The very first person to be killed by East German border guards was Kurt Lieberman, a West German journalist, who had crossed the border in order to talk to some East German farmers that day. This happened not too far from my father's home, about 10 miles I would guess, near Klötze.

Stalin had died in March of 1953. The construction workers in East Berlin, working on those famous buildings on the Stalin Allee, were forever pressured to work faster. The faster they worked, the higher their norms were set. On June 17, 1953, they took to the streets in Berlin against these working conditions and in opposition to communist rule in East Germany. I happened to be in Mühlhausen visiting with my mother. In cities throughout the state, the people in solidarity with the Berlin workers took to the street to organize demonstrations. Such an event took place in the central square in our town and I was on the edge of the crowd, watching these proceedings in wonderment and excitement. The East German police arrived and started to ask the ever-growing crowd to disperse. A dialogue between the people and the police resulted in the disarming of the police. The crowd now became excited.

Then we heard the loud engines of approaching vehicles. From two opposite directions truckloads of Russian soldiers arrived. In a matter of minutes, they dismounted in unison from both sides of the square, built to columns, lowered their rifles with fixed bayonets and then started to trot, not walk, into the crowd. The soldiers now turned to face the crowd, still trotting. As soon as the four columns met, they charged the crowd and in a very short time the crowd was gone.

In Berlin in the meantime, the Russians moved in lots of troops and tanks and did a similar thing as in our town, just on a larger scale, but every much as efficient. This uprising lasted about 3-4 days and in the aftermath, the leaders of the uprising throughout Berlin and East Germany were executed and many people were jailed.

Now the communist regime started to take a strong control over the entire land. More people would be jailed, and business owners lost their factories and shops to the state. The landowners lost their properties and yes, the independent farmer lost his land also. The proclaimed free state of the farmers and workers now became another German nightmare.

Young people, the future cadre of the new German state, had now become members of the communist youth organization called *Freie Deutsche Jugend*, shortened to FDJ. Translated this was known as "Free German Youth." We wore bright blue shirts with the various insignias of rank and achievements. The political indoctrination was now relentless.

We were sent to a youth camp, on the island of Rügen in the Baltic Sea. We had para-military drills and political seminars every day. We also had some fun. We would play soccer or go kayaking. At the same time the world championship games for soccer were played between Hungary and West Germany in the finals. This game was broadcasted over the public address system of the camp. Of course the commentator from the East German state radio would side with communist Hungarians and we all listened in wrapped attention to the development of the game. Well, the Germans scored and the whole camp erupted in a thunderous roar of approval. Every time the Germans charged, we now would cheer. West Germany won the game and became the champion of the world and we would go crazy with excitement. Boy, did we get it the next day! For days the political functionaries had to do damage control and lead us back from the wrong path to the proper way of political thinking.

The radio was a very important link that the people of the east had with the world. The state radio and press obviously reported only what was approved by the party. The news we received about West Germany for instance was totally shaped and reworded to make the west look very bad. The United States was portrayed to us as one of the most evil countries in the world. Similar stories were trumpeted all over the world by a different political group in later decades!

We continued to hear that the United States was run by capitalists and imperialistic politicians, that were treading on the poor working class of America. The United States was using the governments of western European countries to their own advantage in expanding the capitalistic way of life. We were told that the working people in the United States worked very long hours for very low wages. They had no social protection such as insurance and were looking toward the Soviet Union to free them from that awful oppression. Of course the plight of the American "negroes" was totally used to the advantage of the communist system. We would very often see pictures in the cinema or in the press of "negroes" being beaten and hanged by the KKK.

We would try to listen to the radio station RIAS Berlin (Radio in the American Sector). They had a very powerful transmitter and would report to us what was really happening in the world and in our own world. Thanks to the Voice of America! The state government would do anything to disturb these transmissions. The radios you could buy would be constructed to receive only the state radio station. It was announced that altering the radio would be viewed as a crime.

Clandestine radio and other news was a very hot thing and very dangerous, just like in Hitler's time. Of course television was not there yet.

I saw my first TV at the Industrial Trade Fair in Leipzig in 1952. A few students, those who had made good achievements in their studies, would be allowed to go to this Fair in Leipzig and I was fortunate enough to be one of them. We embarked by train and as we left the train station in Leipzig, we saw something we only up to then had heard about. There were people selling newspapers on the plaza, there were vendors selling fruits, oranges and bananas! In the countryside, these items were never available. It was done to impress the many foreign visitors attending the Fair. This was to show them how well the people of East Germany were living. Another blatant lie!

I was sent to East Berlin to attend the annual meeting of the FDJ. Delegations from across East Germany arrived by the thousands to be part of that state sponsored spectacle. We had to attend a rally on the Marx-Engels Platz (the site of the palace of the Prussian King which was destroyed during the war). The leaders of the government spoke to us in glowing terms about the great achievements of the past year and of all the great things awaiting us in the next year. We were very well fed and got to eat things that again were not available in the country. All of this made us wonder why this was happening. When we would ask, they told us that from now on there will be more selective food available. It did not happen.

The Office of the Surveying Services in Erfurt was a corner away from the big state run department store and word would get out that they were selling canned fish, either from

Norway or Poland and we would delegate someone from our ranks, give them money and they would stand in line to buy as many as they were allowed as one individual. We would then split that up; often it was a futile attempt, because there would not be enough to satisfy the requests. Of course it could be other items too, such as toilet paper, always a hot item.

For the next 10 years, food or the lack thereof, was an ever-present important aspect of my life and would continue to be so for some time to come. I received very little money, enough to pay for the rent of the room, but then I needed everything else besides food, such as toothpaste, soap or some clothing. I would start the day with a cup of tea made for me by my wonderful landlord. He would knock on my door to wake me up and a half hour later would knock again and bring the peppermint tea. At lunchtime I would take a walk so that my fellow students would not notice that I had no sandwich to eat. My meals in the evening were quite often slices of rye bread with some mustard spread on it and a cup of tea from the landlord or sometimes just plain water.

There was another phase of life under communism during these times. At harvest time, the farm country needed manual help to bring in the harvests. Private farms had all been confiscated by the state and the acreages had been combined into very large fields. The former owners of these farms had either left or were now just ordinary farm workers. Like all the others in the farm country, they were being paid a monthly salary of some sort. They no longer owned any farm machines either. All machines had been combined in one machine complex, for the purposes of maintenance and security. These machine complexes would then distribute the machines as they were needed. The problem of course was that the machines were very poorly maintained for two reasons. First, the machinists were just ordinary workers, working for a salary and for the state. Second, in East Germany, there were always shortages for just about anything. So machine parts were very scarce. Therefore some of the machines were not in working condition.

Manual labor often came out of the cities and towns, with voluntary workers being recruited. Whole factories and schools were assigned in various regions of the country to work in the fields. We were transported to the farm country and were housed in rooms cleaned up in barns, sleeping in bunk beds on straw mattresses. In the very early morning we were roused up, given a hearty breakfast and then we were trucked, or rode on horse drawn wagons, into the fields. We harvested potatoes or sugar beets, depending on the part of the month. We were put in long rows, a knife in hand, side by side and told to pull each plant by its leafy head and cut the leaves and drop both in place. Behind our row came the gathering/throwing row of workers, they were to gather the beets and throw them onto piles. Wagons would come after them, to pick up the sugar beets. These filled wagons would in turn transport the loads to the side of a railroad track and create huge piles of sugar beets. During one fall, no rail transport ever picked up the sugar beets. The Russian Army at that same time had maneuvers and needed all available rail cars to transport soldiers and material! Frost came and killed the harvested sugar beets. We would work 2-3 days; it was hard work, but the food was good and the farm people appreciated the help.

My mother had moved away from Mühlhausen after the wedding of my sister Traute to Harry Reichel in Schneeberg-Erzgebirge, now called Bad Schlema. Traute and her husband Harry had one son, Peter. My mother lived in a small village with the name of Winterstein south of Gotha in the Thüringer Wald region. She worked as a seamstress, doing work out of her place. She had rented a very small apartment in a house on the outskirts of the village, a very idyllic area of the world. My brother and I visited her about every 4-6 weeks. We took the train to Friedrichroda, the last stop, and then hiked through forests and fields for about 1½ hours. Sometimes we arrived with the last train in the evening; it would be dark already and we had to walk through a forested area. In order to find our way, we had to look up to the sky; that light helped us to find the path. It was pitch dark. We talked a lot on our way and also at times we would sing marching songs or folk songs as we walked along. He and I had always been very close; these times brought us closer together.

In the fall we would go into the forest and cut down trees, drag them home on a handcart and cut them up using a two-man lumber saw. This saw sort of gives a pleasant sound as two people move it back and forth. We split the wood and stacked it in a shed and also provided kindling wood. This would set up our mother for her winter fuel. She cooked and heated with this wood.

Part of my schooling involved taking courses in the science of Geodesy and with that came some actual fieldwork. This consisted of surveying, using triangulations for the map scales of 1:24,000. We went for days into the Harz Mountain, near the border with West Germany. One day we were conducting surveys when we were stopped by two East German border guards. They wanted to know what we were doing there. They said that they had watched us for some time and noticed that we were often straying into West German territory. These were the days before the minefields and death strips. Well, they were satisfied, upon seeing our proper identification and permits.

We also did fieldtrips to teach us how to find our way in strange territories, using just a map and a compass. We did this during the day and also at night. Sometimes we would sleep in a barn by a farmer. We always had a teacher with us, and the ever-present political companion, to make sure we did nothing improper—perhaps escaping to the very near West. One time I was taking a photograph of our group on the platform of a small rail station. All of a sudden, the camera was ripped out of my hands by a soldier. He opened the camera and removed the film, telling me it was against the law to take pictures of rail stations! Another manifestation of the "free world" in the communist system.

I learned a lot about survival in the field and having always been close to nature enjoyed this time very much. We formed some very close friendships and exchanged the thought about our dreams for our future. The human mind does work, no matter the circumstances. The constant shortages of food and consumer goods, coupled with the daily political propaganda from the party started a lot of verbal outbursts and refusals to participate in these political circuses. My brother had married in the meantime and lived about 45 minutes away from me. I was looking forward to my graduation in June 1955.

The political officers in the Institute had all sorts of signs and posters prepared that we were to carry on May 1 during the "spontaneous demonstration" (a forced and organized march of workers through the city). This was designed to show the solidarity of the East German worker with the rest of the enslaved workers of the world. They had painted a caricature of West German Chancellor Konrad Adenauer showing him with blood dripping from his fingernails and the slogan "Stooge of the Americans sucking the blood out of his workers." My brother Wolfgang and I had been selected to carry that sign through the streets. Well, my brother refused and then so did I. Obviously all hell broke loose! What followed next changed our lives forever.

In May of 1955 the country was being prepared to "celebrate" May Day. As members of the Youth Organization, we were all required to wear this button on our shirts.

CHAPTER 5

Refugees Again—Escape from the DDR

Life would never be the same for us. We were immediately separated from our friends and family and a political officer would start a long line of interrogations in order to find out why we behaved that way. Of course we were separated during these interrogations:

"Do you own a radio?" (I did not) "Do you have relatives living in the West?" "With whom are you friends?" "When you are with your friends, are you discussing politics?" "Who is your next door neighbor?" "Who are your brother's friends?" "Does your brother tell you to dislike the state?" "Do you know if you don't answer honestly, that you might not graduate this year?" "Do you like our armed forces?" "Would you volunteer for service in our armed forces?"

Questions like this would be fired at us for hours at a time in meetings with the party officials, for days.

Wolfgang, from the first day of this encounter, noticed that he was being followed at all times after work. My brother now was told that he would have to report to the armed forces on July 1, 1955. They would teach him there to love his country. I was told that right after my graduation I would start my service in the armed forces. The People's Police (*Volkspolizei, VoPos*) were known for their tough service rules. After all, they had been modeled after the Russian Army. In general that means policing the German people, so that they obey the communist rules. My brother and I now started to make plans to flee the country. I visited with my mother one night and Wolfgang stayed wisely back in Erfurt. I told her of our problems. She was to know nothing, for we were sure that the party would pay her a visit.

Luckily, we just had payday. The day was May 14, 1955. We agreed to meet in the evening at the train station. My brother switched into many different streetcars and walked or ran some side streets in order to shake his shadow. At the sta-

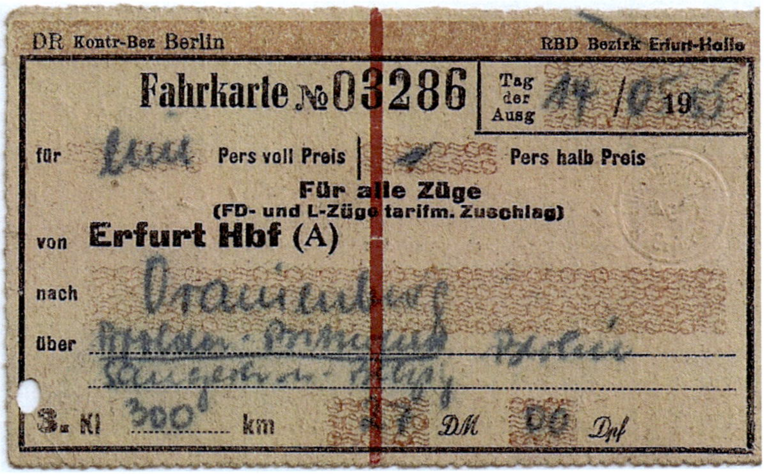

Copy of original RR ticket we had bought.

tion we each purchased a ticket to the town of Oranienburg, a city northeast just outside of Berlin. We had taped our money to the soles of our feet, anticipating a possible search upon entering the Berlin area. We ate a small meal and had one beer in the train snack bar; it could have been our last free one.

I was purposely wearing the FDJ blue shirt with all the proper insignias and some of my achievement medals.

In the morning of May 15, the train was coming into the Berlin administrative area and was halted by the police. There were two East German policemen accompanied by one Russian soldier assigned to look at the passengers of each car. They came to our compartment and asked for the tickets, our passport (East German citizens had to always carry their passports with them at all times, especially when traveling), and the permit allowing us into the Berlin area. We did not have this permit (obviously) and started to fake these guys out. As employees of the "Surveying Office" we were employees of the Department of the Interior and therefore had a very official ID with the seal of the DDR on it. We presented that, I was wearing my uniform shirt and we had tickets not to Berlin but to another city. Well it worked. They left the car and we stood at the window looking at the proceedings. They had ordered out all the passengers of the next car and totally searched that one and strip-searched all the people. Were we lucky!

Later on we pulled into the Berlin station (*Berliner Ost Bahnhof*) and this was to be our point of departure from the train. We knew when the next train in the morning would go to Oranienburg. Now we had to go through another passport and ticket check. We were asked, "You have tickets to Oranienburg, why do you want to get off the train?" We responded, "Well, you see we have an Aunt living not too far from here and since we are here, we thought we would pay her a visit and continue on in the morning." They let us through. We were cartographers, we had studied maps of Berlin and we knew quite well where we were and where we were headed. We had to cross the plaza in front of the station and then go across a bridge spanning the Spree River. The name of the bridge is *"Schilling Brücke."*

The Spree River.

Schilling-brücke *in 2007, looking the way. Wolfgang and I had crossed.*

The bridge belonged to East Berlin. The street on the other side of the bridge was divided, with the West being on the left and the East being on the right. There was an armed guard standing on the East side of the start of the bridge. He stepped in our way as we approached and asked where we were going. We told him the story of the Aunt and also told him the name of the street that we had memorized *(Köpenicker Strasse).* He demanded, "Passports please!" He studied my brother's pass-

East Berlin was to the right.

Köpenicker Strasse looking West.

port and then said, "I know you." When we both heard this our hearts sank. We knew that he was being watched and we thought this would be the end of the line for us! Well, by the luck of the draw or good fortune, the guard said, "You and I have been to school together back in Mühlhausen. Remember, I am so and so? How is the old city?" My brother replied, "What are you doing here?" The guard responded, "They usually pull guards from other cities for Berlin." He then continued, "Well, guys when you cross the bridge, stay to the right and the street you are looking for will be right there, you can't miss it. Just be very careful of the West to the left!"

We proceeded slowly across the bridge, just peeking a little over our shoulders to see what the guard was doing. He was watching us. We talked about what we would do in the upcoming seconds. Once over the bridge, my brother would count to 3 and with the word "NOW" we would in unison dash across the street to the left into West Berlin. And that is what we did. With a last glance at the guard, we saw him standing there. But things went too fast for us to give any thought of us being frightened or worrying about what the guard might do. We just ran like we have never run before!

We kept running, cutting in and out of all kinds of streets, always watching the direction of our run—away from the East! We also paid attention not to run into a West Berlin policeman. We had heard stories of West Berlin police turning fugitives like us back over to the East Berlin police for money!

Our target was a West Berlin police station we had picked out on a map. We went in and announced to the sergeant at the desk, that we were fugitives of East Germany and would like to ask for asylum in West Berlin since we were being hunted. That made it official and we were driven farther into West Berlin and put into a refugee camp for young people. I was under 21 years of age and they did not want to split brothers apart.

The next day we were brought before the West German authorities and asked all the questions pertaining to our claim of being politically harassed by the East. We then were brought before the French military in whose sector we were and they in turn sent us to the British military and there we were kept in a very fancy villa for one week and asked all sorts of questions about our jobs in Erfurt at the Institute. The reason for all this was the fact that we had been working as cartographers on military maps in the East and the various military people started to become very interested in our work. After the Brits were through with us, they turned us over to the American military. They became very serious in their inquiries.

I remember very, very well my first impressions of West Berlin! The stores were filled with all kinds of goods and every

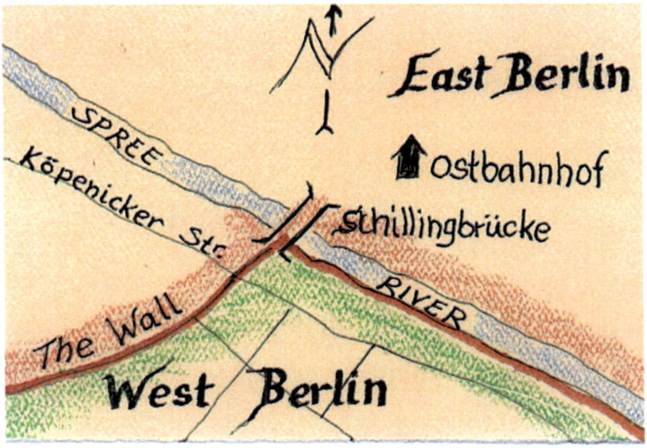

The escape bridge in Berlin.

variety of food. There were restaurants and beer taverns. The best-known beer brand in Berlin to this day is *Schultheiss Bier*, which I will not forget. My brother and I bought a bag full of hard rolls, a can of Sardines and a half-pound of butter. We hid in the high reeds of the Wannsee, away from the other people in the camp. Nobody should know we had any money and we ate this meal in utter delight. This was one of the finer meals of my life!

We spent a total of six weeks in West Berlin and got to know it a little bit. One day the American in charge told us that the next courier plane of the Air Force would fly us out of Berlin to the city of Frankfurt. We were weighed for that process and were told that we were pretty skinny and needed some fat on our ribs! We arrived at the Rhein-Main Airport outside of Frankfurt and were driven by the Army to a CIA (it was known then by another acronym) camp in the Taunus Mountains. The name of the camp was "Camp King." This was our home for the next six weeks. They gave us as much to eat as we wanted and so we started to put some fat on our ribs!

We had been working on military maps for the East German Army, covering the border between the two Germanys. The Russian Army and the East German Army just recently had developed a new symbolization for their maps. U.S. Intelligence was highly interested in learning about that symbolization from us. We transmitted that information with great pleasure. Although, we did understand the implications of our actions! We were now "betraying" military secrets of the Warsaw Pact Nations and thus made us targets to be eliminated.

The camp, located in the Taunus Mountains, was wonderful. In the evening after dinner we could enjoy the great forest air or watch movies and learn all about the USA. We received excellent food and since we were smokers also received free cigarettes. Here is another interesting anecdote. On the first morning, we walked into the breakfast room, sat at a table and watched what people were eating. There were these colorful boxes, like cake mix boxes. People would shake some dried looking stuff into a bowl and then added milk to the bowl and then they started to eat that. We asked our handler, "What is *that*?" And he explained to us, that a lot of Americans eat cereal and milk in the morning for breakfast. We tried it and did not like it. I never ate it again. We stuck to bread, cheese, meat and marmalades. These are still my favorites.

After they heard all they needed to know, we were free to go. The Americans got us a job at the Land Survey Office, located in the northern part of Frankfurt as cartographers. They also gave us enough cash to be able to rent some housing and have money to buy food and other necessities. We got a fresh start and I have forever been thankful to the U.S.A. for that.

May 15 from now on was a day that my brother and I would celebrate as **Liberty Day** every year. Later when I lived in the United States, I called him and we would have a drink. This early time in Frankfurt was of course the years before the Berlin Wall and there was some traffic between the two Germanys. My brother's wife was still in Mühlhausen and she was pregnant at the time. She was in her 4th month of her pregnancy. She turned all their possessions over to her father and boarded a train to Frankfurt. Being visibly pregnant seemed to help. My sister, having been married to her husband Harry in Saxony, was sort of

The West German government issued us the proper Identification Passport that all German citizens had to have under the law.

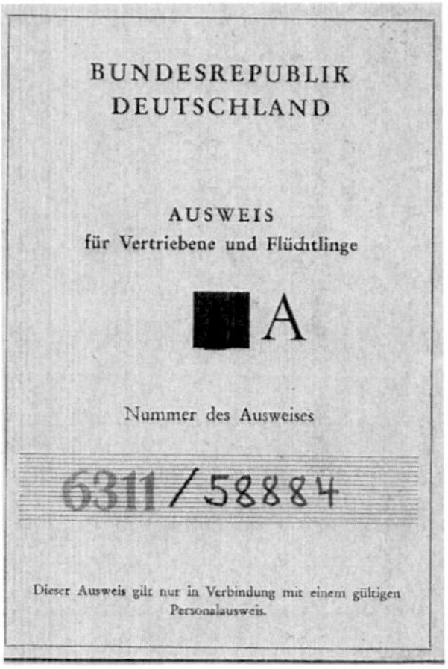

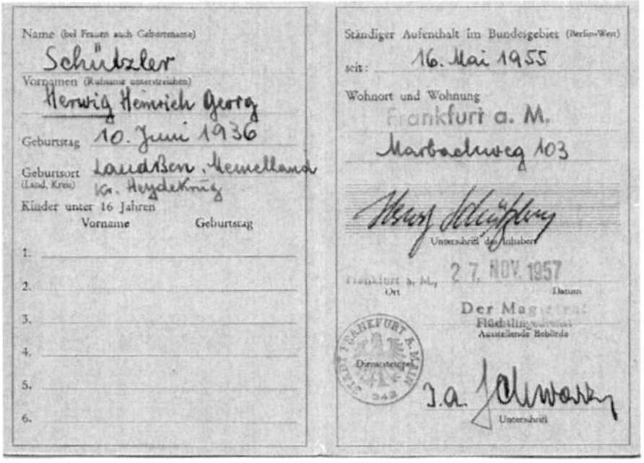

In addition, being part of the forcefully removed German population from the old German provinces, I was issued a document identifying me as Heimat Vertriebener, *a displaced German citizen—a refugee!*

removed from our lives and was not bothered by the authorities and our mother lived all by herself in a small village known as Winterstein in the Thüringer Wald. About two years later, upon our urging she joined us in Frankfurt and found a job as a housekeeper and nanny at an industrialist's household. She was able to travel as she had reached retirement age and the East German government was more than happy to let her go and not be responsible for her pension.

We German refugees were settled into the remnants of Germany, either the East or the West and soon became part of the general population. All refugee camps were eliminated. Now look at the Middle East, especially Israel and the surrounding Arab countries. The United Nations had established Israel in 1947 and Arabs (Palestinians) that did not want to live under a Jewish government left the area and fled into these surrounding Arab countries and were housed in refugee camps. And that is where they still are today! These Arab countries did not assimilate them into their population. Instead they use them as pawns for their political advances. And nobody today, especially the United Nations, says a word about the German refugees of World War II!

I myself enrolled in the "School of Cartography" in Frankfurt in order to prepare for my final exam. Six months later, after some very rigorous written and verbal examinations, I received my diploma as a Cartographer. In the meantime, sort of ironically for us, we worked on almost the same border mapping for the U.S. Army, as we had done for the East before! The Land Survey Office was under the command of the Heidelberg Army Mapping Services, part of NATO and a U.S.

Colonel visited with the office every so often. In 1956 this office became the cornerstone of a brand new German Federal Institution that was being founded at that time. The *Institut für Angewandte Geodäsie* (IfAG) was founded. Translated to Institute for Applied Geodesy. A rather large villa on the south-

Villa Mumm in Frankfurt. Here, at the IfAG, Heidi and I met.

The Marble Hall was my workplace!

The stairs up from entrance.

ern side of Frankfurt, surrounded by a beautiful park-like area was selected for the site. The villa belonged before the war to the Mumm Family, of famous Mumm champagne. The family had donated the property to the city of Frankfurt. Also on the grounds were the quarters of Frankfurt's mounted police and we would often see these horses being trained. They also had horse shows there and it was great fun to see this kind of activity.

My brother was known as big Mr. Schützler and I was known as little Mr. Schützler (*der große und kleine Schützler*)—formal as things go in Germany. I'll elaborate more on this later. I had rented a room in a top floor of a small apartment building from a lady. The room had slanted walls, being like a dormer, and again no heat! In the wintertime I would prepare a pot of tea in my landlady's kitchen and then crawl into the bed and do my homework. I had a washstand that I would fill with water in the evening for my morning wash and would sometimes in the morning find that water frozen. Meals were still a luxury for me. The pay was low; being a refugee meant owning nothing of value, starting with my clothing and whatever I brought with me across the bridge.

We continued to work at the Institute and after a while I got to know some of the people who were my co-workers. Sitting next to my worktable in the Marble Hall sat a female cartographer five years older than me. Her name was Anneliese Michler. She would notice my slightly underweight body and bring me some fruit and things from their garden. She talked to me about her younger sister.

CHAPTER 6

Meeting Heidi and Falling in Love

On a fine day in the month of May (the 22nd) (it was *Wäldchestag* in Frankfurt, the Tuesday after Pentecost) at a company picnic, I was introduced to my future wife Heidi and I will never forget that day. She was the sister of the woman sitting next to me. I saw this shiny, beautiful face, surrounded by the most beautiful blond hair, with a shimmer of gold in it! When I got home that evening, I had to tell somebody, so I mentioned my experience to my landlady and upon hearing my vivid description of Heidi's blond hair she said, "Herr Schutzler, you have fallen in love!" And right she was. Of course I said to myself this can't really happen to me! There will be no chance for me to be able to call this wonderful girl my girlfriend!

Well, fate moves in our lives and Heidi became a cartographic trainee at the Institute and sat near me! I thought, *Can I really be this lucky*? I became scared of my own courage. I would long for Heidi, but at the same time would shy away from her. This went on for some time. The great thing was, Heidi was falling in love with me as well! One day she wrote me a wonderful poem and letter that gave me the needed push to ask her for a date. God, to be in love is one of the greatest things that can befall a human being. The mind dreams the most wonderful dreams and the body urges. At lunchtime we would sit and talk about all kinds of things—music, our work, geography and our daily lives, and our families.

In the meantime Heidi's sister Anneliese started to notice what was going on between the two of us. For some reason (we never really found out why), Anneliese started to tell stories back home to their parents. Stories like Herwig is nothing but a very poor East German refugee; he is not very healthy; he has very bad eyes and one day will go blind; his ears are no good and he also has some sort of heart disease.

I had asked many times to meet with her parents but they would refuse to do so. Heidi's parents then refused to let her ever see me again after work. We would sneak in moments of very short meetings. Heidi was taking singing lessons and she would tell me where that was. I then met her after the lesson and would walk home with her. Her parents found out we were doing that when it took Heidi longer to come home. Now the beatings started. For disobeying the rule not to see me, she would be beaten by her father, by her mother and sometimes in addition by her sister. I would sometimes stand across from their apartment building and look up to the lit up windows and wonder what was going on up there. They lived on the 5th floor. Heidi appeared some mornings with bruises on her face and on her arms and I would become very angry and helpless at the same time. Heidi was underage (19 was underage then) in Germany at that time, so parents still had total authority over their families. I would tell Heidi's teacher what was going on. Fellow students of hers would take notice and also talk with the teacher. His name was Heinz Hoffmann. He would talk with Anneliese, who would deny everything.

Things came to a point where something needed to be done by somebody. Heidi told me she was going to jump from the apartment window to find peace. Heidi and I had a talk and I asked her, if she would marry me, if it could be arranged. Of course Heidi said yes. I said I would file for a hearing before the court in Frankfurt, since she was under the age of 21 and by law not considered an adult. We knew that the repercussions for this move would be very dramatic.

Her parents, Heidi and I were called to a hearing before a family judge. The yelling and screaming at Heidi's house was tremendous, but no hand was laid on her anymore. On the day of the hearing, Heidi and I went from work to the courthouse and waited in a hall for her parents. As they came into the corridor, Heidi's mother started to run towards me with her purse swinging at me. Her father ran after her and stopped this ridiculous nonsense.

The judge first heard my plea and explanations of the beatings and our subsequent asking the court for permission to marry. There was also a letter from the Institute's teacher directing the court's attention to the beatings. Then the judge heard the parents and their reasons for refusal. Then we were dismissed and a few days later an official letter from the family court arrived addressed to Heidi's parents. It informed them that the court saw no reason why we could not marry. The parents were given three weeks to appeal the decision. They never appealed and never brought up the subject of the marriage.

My father, retired by now, was allowed to visit with Wolfgang and me in Frankfurt. The communist government allowed retired citizens to travel to the West, hoping that they would stay there and the state would not need to have to pay their pension. The state always treated a person leaving the state almost as a traitor, threatening no pension. My father heard Heidi sing in the Liebfrauen Kirche in downtown Frankfurt and was very impressed by her voice. He said to me, "Adelheide is a very elegant lady." It was nice to hear that from my Papa.

We became engaged on November 1, 1958. This happened to be my mother's 50th birthday. Heidi took a large arrangement of roses home and her mother promptly threw them out of the window. We posted the wedding to be on March 20, 1959, and

The Römer in 2007. The civil ceremony was held in the Römer in Frankfurt.

Matthäus Kirche *in Frankfurt and view of altar.*

invited all members of the families. Of course there were not that many anyway. My childhood friend Helmut Rennau, who now lived in München, came to be my "best man" and quite a number of people from the Institute showed up for the ceremony. The church we had picked was in the Frankfurt West End, not too far from her parents' apartment. The name of the church is *Matthäus Kirche.* None of Heidi's three family members came to the wedding. Of course my mother and brother were there. We had the wedding "Dinner" at my brother's apartment and then we moved into our first home.

Housing in West Germany at that time was very scarce. We were very happy when we found a furnished room. It was in an old Patrician building with very high ceilings. There were buildings like it that had survived the destruction of the war. The room had a large bed, a small table and two chairs, a wardrobe and a chest of drawers. Cooking was done in a communal type kitchen. The landlord had rented out all the rooms that they could spare. In order for us to go into our room, we had to go through the communal bathroom with shower and tub! Our room used to be a dressing room when the building was owned by the original family. They obviously were a wealthy family. That was an experience and needed some coordination between us and the people that needed to use the bathroom. We all had to make sure to lock both doors when inside it.

One morning, as I was late to go to work, I just walked into the bathroom without first knocking and a fellow renter was standing in the bathtub taking a shower. The bather happened to be female, embarrassment on both sides!

I remember our first meal together. Heidi asked me if I liked ravioli and I had no idea what it was and when she told me, I said great. So we bought ready ravioli in a tin and heated it in a cooking pot. Heidi also told me that her mother did not allow her to be in the kitchen. Not unusual for women of that time. The kitchen was their total domain and what the mother did in the kitchen and what she prepared on food was always under her control. Not even the dominant German male had any influence there. So Heidi had to learn from scratch, starting with how to boil water! I was her first teacher in cooking classes, soon to be taken over by my mother. My mother had always been a good cook and as a housekeeper of late had learned a lot more. To quote my brother in his observation of cooking talents, "Those *Markscheit* women are all dammed good cooks!"

By now Heidi had graduated and left the Institute to take a job at *Ravensteins Verlag* in Frankfurt as a cartographer. They were one of Germany's oldest cartographic firms specializing in hiking maps. This company no longer exists today.

Our earnings were extremely meager, just enough for the rent and the basic things like food. Often we walked, not using the streetcar, since we did not have enough for the fare. We started to look for another place, in order to give us a little more privacy in light of the daily bathroom walk through. We found another, larger furnished room in Sachsenhausen, the other side of Frankfurt across the Main River. Well, now things started to improve! We had a propane gas stove with two burners in the room. That meant we could cook in the privacy of our own "kitchen." Of course in those days nobody cared about safety, as much as we do today. We also had a wood-burning stove so we could heat the room. Trouble was we had no money to buy wood or coal. So most of the time, that stove was cold. The inside of the bed under the covers was much more tolerable and also more fun.

Herwig's Work as Cartographer at the Institute

Interesting things happen in life. As cartographers in communist East Germany, we worked on topographic maps in the scales of 1:25,000 and 1:50,000, covering the border area between the two Germanys. These of course were military use maps, not for public consumption. When I started to draw maps at the Institute, the assignments were military use maps of the border area between the two Germanys (in the same scales as in East Germany!). The Cold War was in full swing at the time. The drafting was still very cumbersome. We engraved the mapping onto specially prepared glass plates and in the evening these plates were moved gingerly into locked steel cabinets for safety! The engraving instrument was developed in Switzerland and this method of "map drafting" was considered the latest technology at the time. There was an individual plate for each layer of a map. For example, there were separate ones for roads, rail lines, drainage, elevation contours, etc. Each plate had on the outside edges "registration marks." The finished plates would be photographed and the registration marks would then help to assure a proper fit when creating print plates.

I developed good skills in drafting and interpreting elevation contour lines. One day my superior asked me if I would be interested in learning the drafting art of shaded terrain for maps. They were in the process of setting up a department of skilled airbrush artists. I was tested and found to be acceptable. A senior cartographer of the Institute had just returned from taking a course of airbrush relief techniques in Geneva, Switzerland, under the tutelage of the world famous Cartographer and Terrain Artist Prof. Eduard Imhoff. Prof. Imhoff had developed a new way of adding light to the sun side of the mountains on a map, by adding an extra yellow tint to that area. I became an Airbrush Terrain Artist and in later years in the U.S.A. I used these skills to earn a living.

I started to look for ways to further my education by attending an engineering school. The Frankfurt School had closed down and there were only two other cartographic schools in West Germany at that time, one in Berlin and one in Munich. Berlin was too close to the communists, so I concentrated on Munich. The problem was I had little money. The government paid for school but not for the cost of living. I applied for all sorts of help and got nowhere fast. I was a refugee without resources to help me along a very ridiculous bureaucratic path. No doors were opened for me anywhere, also I observed other people with the right connections get what they wanted. And of course the old "class system" of Germany was again in place. So, I had to give up this dream.

Heidi always had trouble with her tonsils. So one day she got ill again, with fever and a swollen throat and needed medical help. We went to the doctor and sat in his office what seemed to be hours. Finally, Heidi got examined and he decided to do some cutting right in his office. He cut out whatever was left after Heidi's last operation, her adenoids. Afterwards Heidi was lying on a couch in the office for a while, until the worst of the bleeding stopped and then we were sent home. Again we had no money for a taxi so I tried my very best to get Heidi home, half carrying her and half coaxing her along. In our cold place she went to bed.

Heidi's parents cared less what was happening to us. There was no help whatsoever from them. My mother came by carrying in a shopping bag, some wood and coal and we lit a fire in order to warm the room a little. Such is life in the glorious socialized system, where health insurance cost so very little and all services free for the masses of the people! How people get fooled. Years later, while I was visiting in Germany, I needed the help of an eye doctor. I called in and was asked if I was a private patient or a social system patient. I told them I was a visitor from the U.S. and therefore would pay cash. When I arrived at the doctor's office I was directed to a special door, not the regular door marked "patients," and got immediate attention and service. The system works! The Democrats of the 1990s and 2000s please listen!

Soon we bought our first piece of furniture—a piano! First things first, we wanted to make sure that Heidi's voice did not get rusty. The piano was an old upright, a pitch-black monster, not badly tuned. I was on the bottom of the government pay scale and Heidi on the bottom end in the private mapping industry. There was no help from Heidi's family and my mother was a housekeeper, living in the Frankfurt household of her employer. Refugees with no connections got nowhere. We were told that there was no chance for us to be able to get a real apartment. Again, one would have to have connections.

I started to get restless, seeing that Germany was not the place to get us financially ahead.

I applied at the South African Automobile Association in Johannesburg and they offered me a job. The only problem was that they would not pay for our airfare to go down there, or at least advance it. Heidi told me if I wanted to go to South Africa, I would have to go without her. The ANC (Mandela's Anti-Apartheid Group) at that time gave the whites a lot of trouble and quite a few people got killed.

At about that time, the International Cartographic Association held their annual meeting in Switzerland and they came to the Institute for a side trip. There was my chance! I approached the American delegate, Mr. Duncan Fitchet, and asked for a meeting with him. He was then the General Manager of Rand McNally's cartographic division in Skokie, Ill., near Chicago. He listened with great interest and asked me to forward an application to his attention. My life was now taking another fundamental turn.

The head of the Institute at the time was Prof. Erwin Gigas, one of the leading German Geodesists. Only in much later years did I discover that he was very instrumental in helping the American military in their search for geodetic information. (See *Smithsonian* magazine, Nov. 2019 issue on the subject.) Prof. Gigas encouraged me to go to the United States. I am sure he did talk with Mr. Fitchet. At the end, I got a nice letter from Dr. Gigas upon my departure from the Institute.

Heidi and I discussed this planned move at length and I also of course discussed it with my mother and brother. We decided that I should apply. And so I did send the application, together with some samples of my work to Rand McNally in Chicago. The samples included examples from my terrain relief art. An offer was made to us. They offered a full-time job to me for two years, they would advance the airfare to Chicago, and they also offered Heidi a job so that we would be able to pay back that advance.

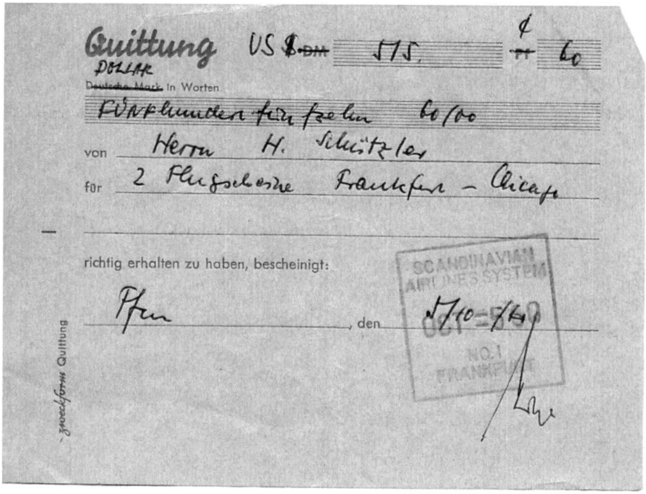

Quittung US $ ~~DM~~ 515. ¢ ~~Pf~~ 60

DOLLAR ~~Deutsche Mark~~ in Worten Fünfhundert fünfzehn 60/00

von Herrn H. Schützler

für 2 Flugscheine Frankfurt – Chicago

richtig erhalten zu haben, bescheinigt:

, den

SCANDINAVIAN AIRLINES SYSTEM NO. 1 FRANKFURT

Zweckform Quittung

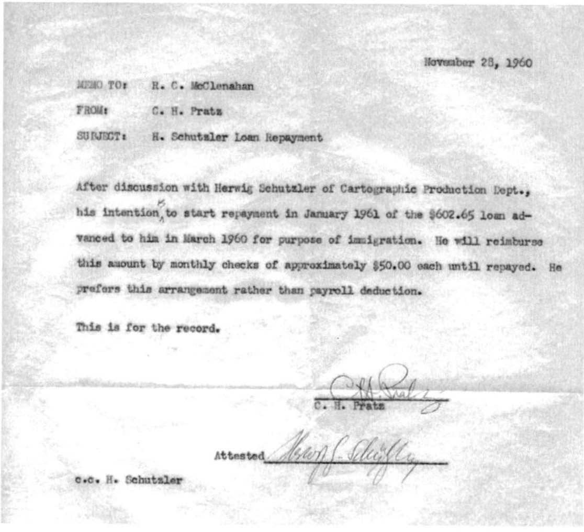

November 28, 1960

MEMO TO: R. C. McClenahan

FROM: C. H. Pratz

SUBJECT: H. Schutzler Loan Repayment

After discussion with Herwig Schutzler of Cartographic Production Dept., his intention is to start repayment in January 1961 of the $602.65 loan advanced to him in March 1960 for purpose of immigration. He will reimburse this amount by monthly checks of approximately $50.00 each until repayed. He prefers this arrangement rather than payroll deduction.

This is for the record.

C. H. Pratz

Attested

c.c. H. Schutzler

A receipt of the advance money.

Now came another bureaucratic hurdle from the American side. I was born in a German region that was now officially the territory of Lithuania. Therefore under the U.S.A. Immigration Quota System at the time, I was classified as being born in Lithuania. What a ridiculous nonsense! Under that system, they allowed only so many "Lithuanians" per year into the U.S.A. The quota was filled for years! There was of course a loophole (what else is new). Heidi, my wife, was born in Frankfurt, "proper" Germany. Lo and behold they now looked at us in the light of the German quota and there the numbers were plentiful. Voilà, no more problems.

Next came the filling out of very long questionnaires from the immigration officials. Then we went to meet officials in the American Consulate General in Frankfurt, where we had meetings and were questioned about our sincerity, moral character and me in particular about any possible communist connections. These meetings took place on various days. I became restless, knowing that Rand McNally was waiting for us. Finally, we were issued the final documentation to be accepted into the United States of America.

Well, how easy it is today to come to the States! As a matter of fact, the illegal immigrants want "their rights" protected! And a lot of the legal Asian immigrants don't even have to pay income taxes for five years! How did Hillary put it, "We have to do it for the common good." Please watch out for politicians that say, "We will protect all people and all the rich have to give to the poor. Everything for the common good." That is what the communists said to us. Problem is, when there are no more rich people, where is the money coming from to pay for all that? Raise the taxes to no end; the State will take care of all your needs . . .

It was time for us to leave Germany and start a new chapter in our life in the United States of America. The day to leave Germany and our families was moving closer and closer. We each had one suitcase to pack, containing things we thought we needed immediately upon our arrival in a strange country. That was a very difficult undertaking, to say the least! I thought shirts, pants, socks and underwear, besides a toothbrush, deodorant or shaving needs were the important things to start.

There was one more legal thing we had to do, before we could depart, we had to go to the local police and register leaving our current address and stating where we were moving to.

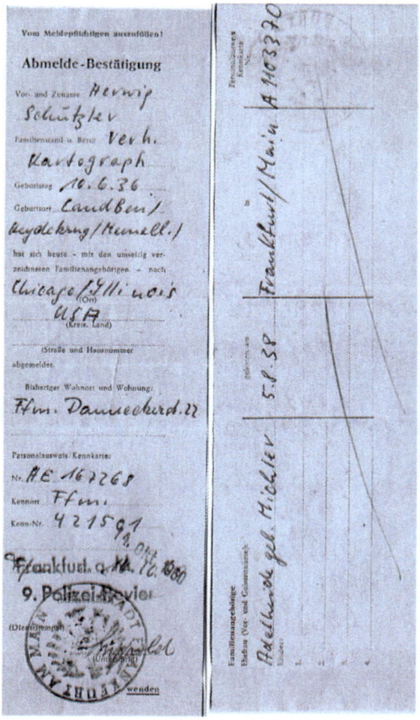
Vom Meldepflichtigen auszufüllen!

Abmelde-Bestätigung

Vor- und Zuname Herwig Schnitzler

Familienstand u. Beruf verh. Kartograph

Geburtstag 10.6.36

Geburtsort

hat sich heute – mit den umseitig verzeichneten Familienangehörigen – nach

Chicago/Illinois (Ort)

USA (Kreis, Land)

(Straße und Hausnummer

abgemeldet.

Bisheriger Wohnort und Wohnung:

Personalausweis/Kennkarte:

Nr. AE 167268

Kennort Ffm.

Kenn-Nr. 421591

Frankfurt a. M.

9. Polizei-Revier

(Dienststempel)

(Unterschrift)

wenden

Above: This is one of our two suitcases we discarded, when we moved out of Surrey Drive in 2017.

Left: Registration to leave Germany.

CHAPTER 7

Heidi's Story in Her Own Words

Adelheide (Michler) Schutzler

I was born on August 5, 1938, as the 2nd daughter of Alfred Michler and his wife Sophie (Schuchmann) Michler. Alfred was one of 9 children. The ninth child was stillborn. My father was born in Brieg in 1901, near Breslau (Warzlaw) in former German Silesia. This area is now part of Poland since the end of WWII. He was the oldest son of the coal miner Hermann Michler and his wife Rosina Hermansa. Alfred lived in poverty, lost his father in 1915, a soldier on the French front at the time, which made the 14-year-old Alfred the "man of the house."

He was not allowed to receive a higher education as a member of the "lower class," a fact he resented all his life. He was an extremely intelligent, self-educated man. He entered an

Alfred Michler's stamp he used on his correspondence.

apprenticeship as a chimneysweep and became a wandering tradesman. That was a requirement of the various tradesmen guilds at the time. He reached Frankfurt/Main, where he met my mother Sophie and he married her June 28, 1928.

My mother Sophie was born in 1904 and was one of 8 children. She was the daughter of the tool and dye maker Jakob Schuchmann and his wife Sophie Petri, who was a midwife. They both died very young in their forties, within one month of each other. My grandfather died of stomach cancer and my grandmother of TB that she had contracted from one of her patients. This left the children orphans. Sophie was only 13 years old and had to go through many hardships as an abused household helper—hard physical labor, bloody hands from doing laundry by hand and no laws to protect children!

Alfred married Sophie when she was 24 years old in Frankfurt/Main, where she had worked as a housekeeper and nanny. On November 3, 1931, their first daughter Anneliese entered this world and I came along seven years later. I was supposed to be a son (according to my father's wish) and this disappointed him so much, that my poor mother never received the promised reward (a fur coat) for giving birth!

My memories start very early. I see myself standing in my crib with the light coming in under the door, screaming, because I wanted to join my parents and sister on the other side of the door since they were still awake!

The first two years of my life were happy and secure, even though WWII had started in 1939. Frankfurt was not affected

What is that light?

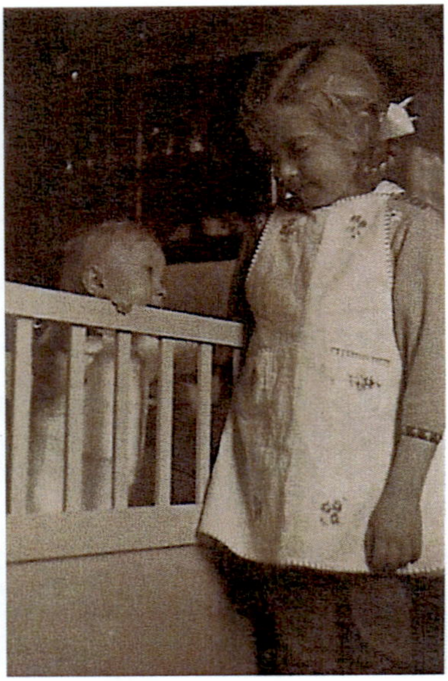

Happy to see sister Anneliese.

in the beginning. As the war progressed, the bombings started in 1942. We had to run down from the 5th floor, day or night, into the basement of the apartment building we lived in. There were rats in the basement, looking for food. They were extremely aggressive, capable of jumping at a little girl's throat. I can still see their beady eyes! The other choice we had were the official air raid shelters, quite a distance away. While running in the streets, some of the Allied planes would fly over, close to us (called *Tiefflieger* in German) and try to kill the fleeing women, children and old people with rapid gunfire. To this day, the sound of sirens and the drone of an airplane's propellers give me goose bumps and a stomachache. We were cold; there was very little wood or coal to heat the apartment. My sister and I tried to secretly steal square pieces of tarred wood that had been used to pave road sections close to the streetcar tracks. Had we been caught, we would have been severely punished. Any affront against the Nazi regime was punishable by death or imprisonment, regardless of the age of the offenders.

We were very hungry and had very little food available for us to eat. I vividly remember my mother standing in line for hours for food, only to be sent away because they had run out. She fainted one time from hunger. She gave most of the food to her children. I tried to find water or a few ice chips for her, but no one would help. I can still see the pain in her face and wanted to make the hurt in her face go away. Once I was able to do this and it still fills me with pride today. While she was patiently standing in line, I became bored and started exploring nearby. Behind a stone wall I discovered a pile of half-rotten potatoes. I quietly walked away and did not say a word until we were out of earshot of the others, because I knew there would have been a stampede. When we were safe, I told my mother about my find. She waited until nobody saw her, then she gathered the potatoes, took them home, salvaged the good parts and we had the best feast of potatoes boiled in water with a little salt! I was so proud that I had made my mother happy. To this day, I cannot throw away an old piece of bread.

My father was ordered into the Army in 1943 as a 42-year-old man. Ironically, he hated the Nazis. He was sent to the Western Front to fight the French as a specialist in mine placement. He was captured and became a POW. After the war ended, he and the other prisoners were ordered to remove the unmarked mines. Many of his fellow soldiers, some of them younger than 18 years of age, were blown to bits right beside him. We at home had no idea where he was or if he was still alive. When he finally returned, I did not recognize him when he rang the doorbell. I must have broken his heart. He was a changed man, with a broken soul from all the horror he had witnessed. Over the years he drank himself to death, trying to forget. He died in May 1967, never to enjoy a retirement.

One other incident is engraved in my mind forever. My mother, sister and I were on a train to take Anneliese to a country home (Landheim) for school-age girls located north of the city in the Taunus Mountain. She was 12 or 13 years of age, which made me about 6 years old. The train stopped suddenly and we were ordered out of the cars. Strafing fighter planes were attacking the train. We all tried to find the nearest ditch, flattened ourselves into the dirt and hoped for the best. While we were frightened for our lives, some evil people remained behind on the train, went through people's possessions and stole my sister's violin out of a large basket. It also contained her linens and clothing. My mother apparently had not hidden it well enough. I was the saddest of us all, because I had hoped to learn to play violin, like my big sister!

Playing the violin would have been impossible. I cut my left hand very badly when I was playing with some bottles and fell. It was 1944 and my friend Erika and I had played "house" on a sidewalk. I had to fill a glass bottle from a public waterspout (they were opened for people who were bombed out) and suddenly the sirens started blaring to announce ANOTHER air raid. I started running towards home, tripped and cut both hands badly. The cuts were on my left hand directly under the middle finger and also my right wrist. To this day I have a stiff and atrophied finger as a reminder of that day. When I fell and got cut, the blood was squirting out but I had a guardian angel even then. I fell directly in front of the Red Cross Chapterhouse! The EMT's chased after me, bandaged me up and told me to hold my hands above my heart. My poor mother, who normally never left me, had gone this once without me to check the rumor, that some coal was available. She came back to find her little daughter all messed up! I had worn a green *Loden* (coat) that was now brown from all the blood. She took me to the hospital, where they gave me chloroform in order to sew my hands. This was my first surgery of many different ones to come in my life. I still can smell the strong odor of the chloroform. On the way home, we had to dodge another air raid and then stayed in the shelter for days. I was hungry, cold and full of pain.

Days later I got another life experience—realizing that my pain was nothing compared to the agony a Russian lady had to endure during surgery without any anesthesia. They would not waste any precious medication that was still around on an enemy. I had to listen to her cries, while I was waiting to have my sutures removed. Great experience for a five year old! No wonder I hate hospitals and get a stomachache every time that I have to enter one.

I saw my first dead person as a six year old. Two German soldiers, armed with a machine gun, had tried to hold off advancing American infantry around the railroad station in Frankfurt. They didn't make it. First I saw a machine gun, covered with a bloody army coat and then the owner of that coat a few yards further, dead on the pavement. We turned around, mother tried to protect my sister and I from the sight, but as we walked back on the other side of the street, there was the second dead soldier.

I will always remember the waxen color of his hands. Thankfully his face was covered. You mature very quickly in war!

It was daunting to exist at this time. I was so hungry I cannot describe the pain I had in my belly. Then there were bombs destroying half of the large apartment complex above us. While the grown-ups were crying and praying around us, I was cold, scared and wanted to be able to ease my mother's pain and anguish. She was such a strong, brave person that never thought of herself, but I knew how much she suffered for her children and missed her husband. She divided the meager food between my sister and I by weighing it on a letter scale and took nothing for herself.

Once I felt like a hero. After an air raid, we went up to our apartment on the 5th floor and as I ran ahead I found a

This is what Frankfurt looked like from the air at the end of the war!

phosphorous bomb on the steps. It had not detonated. If you poured water over those things, they would not go out, but it made it worse. Mother found a bucket full of sand that was always handy for that purpose and smothered it. I had saved the building, and all the neighbors began calling me "guardian angel" and "our sunshine." I was the proudest little six year old you ever saw! On the day of the German surrender, American GI's came into our street. I remember my mother crying tears of joy, because the war was finally over.

The Americans introduced me to my first banana. I tried to eat it with the skin on—I did not know you had to peel it! I had never seen such a fruit. German children would beg from the GI's in the streets for gum and candy. We were strictly forbidden by our mother to humble ourselves like that; she threatened to beat us to within an inch of our lives! Only once did my sister Anneliese, who was 14 years old at the time, disobey her. I was lying on the couch with a very high fever from tonsillitis. I could not swallow or talk; my throat was so infected and swollen. Here comes my sister with a piece of cinnamon-flavored gum she had begged from a soldier. This could have put her in grave danger. There had been cases of rape of girls her age by some American GI's. Bad Nazi's, you know! Mother just yelled a little and then I was allowed to chew my present. We all know how spicy that stuff is, well it helped break open my puss-filled throat and healed my infection in one day! I could see that my mother was glad that Annneliese had disobeyed her.

The Americans gave me my first "real" doll. Until then I had a rag doll my mother had made from old silk stockings

Alfred Michler carved the heads as a POW in France and Sophie Michler made the bodies.

and a doll whose head my father had carved as a prisoner of war for each of his daughters. When he came back, mother made the bodies and dresses. They are here with me in Lancaster, a treasure beyond words.

When the war was finally over in 1945, I could start school. I loved it and only got slapped once (corporal punishment was allowed and used often in those days). I had to read out loud and kept mispronouncing the name "Erwin" repeatedly. Obviously, I never married an Erwin!

In the fourth grade we had to take an entrance exam if we wanted to go to high school. A child could go to grammar school until the eighth grade and stop or go to middle school to age 15 or choose higher education—but only after being deemed bright enough to attend a school. I passed the exam with flying colors and entered *Bettina Schule, Realgymnasium für Mädchen* (an exclusive girls' school) in the 5th grade. This was quite an accomplishment for a daughter of a mere chimneysweep. Most other girls were from wealthy families of doctors, lawyers and others. It takes eight years to graduate, so you go to school for 13 years before entering college or the university.

I loved school until I reached eighth grade when I became the target of a sadistic social studies teacher. She used to pick

Anneliese, my Mutti *Sophie, and me in Taunus, 1951.*

Alfred & Sophie Michler, September 1964.

one girl from each class and pin her against a wall after each lesson. She came closer and closer into your face with her thick nearsighted eyes, boring into yours until your tears started flowing, then she let you go. She should have been fired, but in those days your parents thought you were guilty of whatever, so you got more punishment at home! Besides, some gossip was around that she was the lesbian partner of the principal and therefore you were on her hit list as well!

During those years I made my *Frei Schwimmer* (swimming level). I had loved the water since I was very young; I even tried to swim in puddles in the summer. My father was a strong swimmer and he taught me the basics by tying a bicycle inner tube around my waist and throwing me into the Nidda River (tributary to the Main River) in Frankfurt. I trusted him completely and obviously was not mentally "damaged" by this unorthodox treatment! I progressed to Red Cross lessons, passed Swimmer and turned into a dedicated aquatic person all my life. During my years in aquatics as an instructor, I must have helped thousands of children and adults love the water, including Herwig. At the age of 43 he became my proudest student when he learned to swim with dolphins and whales in the ocean after he stopped being scared.

My singing voice was "discovered" by my music teacher in high school and he begged my parents repeatedly to let me study voice. It was discovered that I had this very high coloratura soprano, which I still have today at the age of 77! My father and my mother relented, but also insisted that I pick up a decent profession as a back-up. Since my sister was a cartographer, I also chose to become a cartographer. I started to get solo singing engagements in Frankfurt. Many professional musicians told me that I had a rare gift and should concentrate to become a professional singer. I even passed an exam of the Opera House in Frankfurt, to see if I was suitably talented to succeed. I was told not to marry for some time to prevent interference of my developing career!

What did I do? I met this skinny, young man with a deep voice and beautiful slender hands one day while I was visiting my sister at the *Institut für Angewandte Geodäsie.* She worked there as a cartographer, next to this young man. He was a poor refugee from communist East Germany and she brought him fresh fruit from our garden. This meeting changed my life completely! That fateful day, I found a field mouse being tortured by a cat and I of course had to rescue the poor thing. The young man bent down and helped me. That did it! Bingo! It took him one whole year to bring up the courage to ask me for a date. Talk about being shy! We kissed for the first time on June 19, 1957, on the bank of the River Main.

Now the real trouble started. My parents did not want me to date a poor refugee with extremely thick glasses. They thought he surely would go blind very soon! They did not even bother to meet with him, but took my sister's word for it. She did not take it kindly that her little sister found a guy, while she did not even have a boyfriend at 26 years of age! Could it have been jealousy?

My parents tried to beat me into submission when I tried to sneak out for a movie or stay at a ping-pong game at the Institute after classes. I remember one real bad incident. I was singing a solo at a church and as I looked down into the audience, I saw Herwig and a few rows behind him my father! It took all my strength to finish my oratorio and on the way home, I heard my father coming up behind us, slapping Herwig's arm off my waist and threatening to beat him up. Herwig stayed calm and went home with the streetcar. I refused to talk to my father; oh how I hated him then!

I came to work or to school with black and blue marks all over my body, including my face. My teachers threatened to press charges against my parents. Finally, Herwig said that is enough. He and I talked about getting married, way ahead of what we had planned to do. Since I was only 19 years old, I could not marry without parental consent at the time—one had to be 21 years of age. With a heavy heart, Herwig and I filed for court permission to marry. After weeks of legal steps and mental hell at home (at least the beatings had stopped), we received the court's permission to go through with the marriage.

We were legally married on March 20, 1959, before a Justice of the Peace in the famous Frankfurt Römer. And on March 21, 1959, in the *Matthäuskirche* (located on Friedrich-Ebert-Anlage) we had our church wedding. Herwig's small family, and friends and colleagues from the Institute were in attendance. I was a very sad bride, because my parents and my sister never showed up!

Wedding at the Matthäus Kirche. *Roland as ring bearer and flower boy.*

Herwig's mother helped me make my wedding gown, his sister-in-law made the meal and baked a cake for us, and we celebrated at their small apartment. Our honeymoon was spent in a furnished, rented room that was to be our home from now on. Four or five other people shared the same kitchen, toilet and bathroom! That made for an interesting first year of married life. In order to reach our room, we had to go through the communal bathroom that had a tub in it. The toilet was in a separate room. One morning Herwig rushed to work—without first knocking on the bathroom door—and there stands a lady in the tub, sans clothing! Good Morning! That made us look for another rented room, as apartments were not to be found and out of our financial reach even if available.

The next rented room we found had a bed, a bathtub with a water heater, and a propane cooking stove—all in one room! We also bought a used, upright black piano to add to the living quarters. Cozy! I tried to continue my voice and piano lessons, but my heart was not in it. My health was also not the greatest and I had to have my adenoids removed that were missed in two previous tonsillectomies! Herwig took me to the doctor's office, where I had to sit in a chair to be anesthetized with chloroform. When I woke up, I was bleeding from my nose and mouth. At least I did not have to sit on my hands strapped into a chair and have the doctor yank out the tonsils, as was the case the first two times!

After this ordeal, Herwig took me home on foot. I insisted that I was strong enough to walk the mile, since we did not have enough money for a cab. Those were the good old days, which built character! What hurt more than any physical pain was the lack of interest of my parents. They did not even call to hear if I was ok. They hated Herwig that much for taking their little girl away. Herwig's mother came and brought food and some wood and coal for our stove to heat the room.

This pitiful situation led to Herwig's desire to leave Germany for another country in order to give me a better life. He promised me a house with a garden full of flowers and trees and he kept his word! He met with the General Manager of Rand McNally in Chicago, who was at a conference in Switzerland. He told Herwig to apply and he was accepted. Rand McNally agreed to loan us $600 for the airfare and on October 17, 1960, we left our country to start a totally new life. It was very hard for me. I was terribly homesick for more than 12 years, even though my parents did not accept my husband. I remember the flight from Frankfurt to Düsseldorf to Kopenhagen to New York as if it was yesterday, not 47 years ago. The heartache of leaving the only home I ever knew, the thrill of flying and seeing wonders like Greenland from the air and then the terror of landing in New York not understanding the language, was a lot to handle.

In school they had taught me the "King's English," a *wonderful* preparation for understanding American slang, especially black porters and service people! While waiting for and missing our connection to Chicago, we decided to get a cup of coffee. When they automatically also served us a glass of water, we were petrified it would cost extra money and we would not have enough. After sitting around for some hours, someone noticed the two lost souls, looked at our tickets and finally put us on another flight to Chicago! Eckart Leistikow, by previous arrangement, had waited patiently at the airport to pick us up. A true friend! We are still friends with him and his wife Lotti, aka "Lisa," after 47 years. The first few weeks in America were spent in a rented efficiency apartment in the Ridgeview Hotel in Evanston, IL, for $8 a day. We were in heaven! A whole apartment with a bed, a living room and a bathroom! That first night in America, on October 17, Herwig and I experienced our first shower—together! Until then, we only knew bathtubs. We even had a refrigerator. Later we realized, it was a very basic boarding house, but we were so easy to please then. Through Eckart's managing and with the help of some other German immigrants, we found a nice permanent apartment on the north side of Chicago on Paulina Street; it became our first real home.

We were extremely poor. We had to pay off the $600 loan to Rand McNally. Herwig was paid $2.20 per hour and I was paid $1.65 per hour until we had paid off the loan; then Rand McNally let me go. Husband and wife were not allowed to work in the same department back then. How times have changed! Immigrants now have a much easier time to come here. We had to go through a very long process. They did not want to let Herwig come into the country, because his place of birth was then communist Lithuania, with a very low quota range. Only my marriage to him moved him up on the quota ladder. I was very sad that I inadvertently helped him to go to America, because I did not want to go. Life can be funny at times! The first few months were brutal. I was homesick, we were poor, we had a foreign language to learn, and we didn't really know anybody. Here is one example. I came down with a bad bladder infection, with blood in my urine. After days of pain someone made an appointment with their doctor for me. We took the elevated train or "L" to that office and sat for a long time in the waiting room. We had no idea what to do next. Nobody helped us and after what seemed hours, we left and went home. I never got help from that doctor! I can't even express the frustration and the pain that caused.

After living six months in America, I did not want to wait any longer to start a family. I wanted a child very badly as a sign of our love for each other. When I found out in 1961 that I was pregnant, I was thrilled. I loved this little person inside me more than I could ever express. When it was finally time for him to enter this world, he wasn't sure he wanted to leave that warm, loving place in which he had spent nine months. It took some hard pushing and pulling with forceps, and after 2½ days of labor, Michael Thomas Schutzler entered the world on January 6, 1962, at the Evanston Hospital. All this happened during a blizzard. This kind of love, only a mother can experience. The love when she holds her newborn child in her arms for the first time. This joy and love can never be taken away, no matter how much your child grows up and comes under the influence of others. I can still feel the warm little body in my arms and when things get tough sometimes, I think of that. I will always love my sons with all my heart . . .

Shortly before Mike's birth, we had moved into a larger apartment at 1542 Birchwood Avenue in the Rogers Park neighborhood in Chicago. Our landlord was a policeman. His wife Linda was my age and became my best friend. She helped me with Mike, since she had more experience with babies. She had married Paul, who had three children from a previous marriage, and she had three more with him. She taught me many words in English and showed me how to apply make-up, since Herwig was very old fashioned and opposed to make-up and low-cut dresses and shorts! She explained to him that we lived in America now and a wife had some rights!

As it turned out, her rights were violated in the worst way!

Sadly, she was killed by an assassin in 1969. I often wonder what became of Linda's children?

Mike was born with a closed membrane from tear duct to nasal cavity. On February 1, 1962, at less than one month old, I had to hold him in my lap while a female eye surgeon opened the canal by pushing a crooked needle through! I can still hear his screams and feel the pain that went through my body for him. Then we took the bus home. We did not have a car or the money for a taxi! The doctor's fee had to be paid by us as well—there was no health insurance at that time for working people. Herwig made about $2.20 per hour, which was barely enough for us to live on.

Mike was a colicky baby, making it very tough on new parents at times. I remember Herwig and I sticking our heads out of the window and closing the window as close above our necks as we could, in order not to hear the constant screams from Mike. We had tried every remedy people were suggesting to us, including paregoric, but nothing seemed to help. What was the doctor's advice? Bear with it! We had no family to help out nor could we afford a baby sitter. On Mother's Day 1962, Mike slept through the night for the first time. What a wonderful present for his *Mutti*!

Herwig took his driver's test on July 17, 1962, after Paul had taught him to drive a car. Shortly after that we bought a 1953 Chevy Bel Air from a colleague for $50.00 and we felt like millionaires, because we now could go for drives! We even sanded off the ugly mustard paint job and repainted it turquoise on the driveway of our good friends Eckart and Lotti in Wheeling. I got my own driver's license on July 8, 1963, at the age of almost 25!

Then my parents paid for the ticket for a flight to Frankfurt for Mike and me. They wanted to see their first grandchild. My father, who had a badly deteriorated hip joint at that time and was in constant pain, was crawling on all fours with his grandson. He always wanted sons and my own birth had really disappointed him at the time. Now I made up for it. We had a great visit, which made it very hard to go back to Chicago, into almost poverty. I was so very homesick for my family in those years. I was torn between the love of my home country and my husband. It took me almost 20 years and the statement of my almost grown sons, to accept the fact that I was to be an American and no longer German. I became an American citizen in 1980. But in my heart and traditional values I will always remain Deutsch!

Mike grew and developed well. He was a happy, inquisitive and very intelligent little boy. He loved the water even then; he enjoyed going into Lake Michigan with his Mom. We were so proud of him that we decided to have one more like him.

In July 1964 I realized that a sibling was on the way. The pregnancy was just as great as the first with Mike. I always felt super when pregnant, but boy did I pay for it in the end! I had some early contractions on March 14, then on the 16th more contractions, but my water did not break until early in the morning on the 20th. We were awakened by a wrong number call and the water gushed out. We got into the car, with a thick towel between my legs and drove many miles to the Arlington Heights Hospital. My doctor was a German physician. I felt safe with him. He turned out to be an alcoholic, who had been fired from another hospital for that reason. One learns a lot in retrospect! He was too hung over to attend to me and showed up after Peter was delivered by a resident on duty, who did a good job. Of course during labor from 5:15 a.m. until 4:28 p.m. when the little guy came out, I had no pain medication since the doctor was not present to give the OK! Thanks a lot. Herwig still remembers my screams through the walls.

Peter Henry Schutzler, our second son, was a healthy, happy and peaceful baby with no colic. It was wonderful! Mike loved his little brother from the start and they remained very close until adulthood. Herwig worked many hours doing different jobs during those years, which made it even harder for this lonely stay-at-home mom. No family, no car, marital problems at times, the loneliness and homesickness was very difficult to bear.

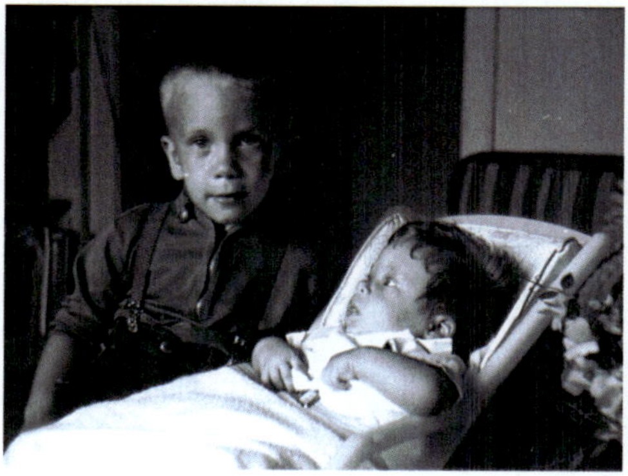

Mike has a brother, Peter Henry Schutzler (1965).

To make matters worse, I grew an ovarian cyst, which was 5" x 10" on my left ovary. We were on our first real, short vacation trip in southern Illinois. I swam in the hotel pool and played with my two boys in the water, when I suddenly felt a large mass on my left side. On our return I found out the diagnosis. Immediate surgery was needed, due to the twisted mass of the cyst. On the day of my admittance to the hospital, Herwig found a letter in the mailbox stating that our health insurance (with Metropolitan Life) had been cancelled. They claimed that there was a preexisting condition and therefore it was not covered. Great! The gynecologist offered to make the fee real reasonable, if I wanted. I was so naive, until he came closer and closer to examine me when it hit me what he meant! What a pig! The surgery was pretty painful and when I came home I had to go back to regular chores, like changing Peter's diapers. I did that on the floor, since I was not allowed to lift him. My two boys had missed me terribly while I was in the hospital, they did not want me to leave again. Back then, hospital stays took many days. A bond between mother and children is very special and forever, even if boys grow into men and sometimes let strangers interfere with this precious gift. My life was now filled with a lot of work and responsibilities; raising the children became my primary path in life.

Here ends Heidi's story in her own words.

CHAPTER 8

Immigrants in the U.S.A.

Our official day for our "Green Card" was October 17, 1960. We were two very young people, each carrying one medium-size suitcase constructed out of laminated cardboard, and this is how we arrived.

We had tickets with SAS Airlines and first went to Copenhagen, Denmark, and then on to New York. As we approached North America, I saw the northern light phenomena shaped like a crown and took it as a good omen. Heidi, unfortunately, was plagued with very bad earaches. After customs and immigration clearance at the Idlewild (now Kennedy Airport) in New York, we were then to board a plane to Chicago. But there was a problem of some significance. I spoke no English and Heidi had mastered a terrific Shakespearean English from her school days. We sat there in these corridors and listened to some announcements on the public loudspeakers, not understanding a thing! And we knew there was a man in Chicago at the airport to pick us up. What could we do? We must have sat there for hours. We remember one businessman in a gray

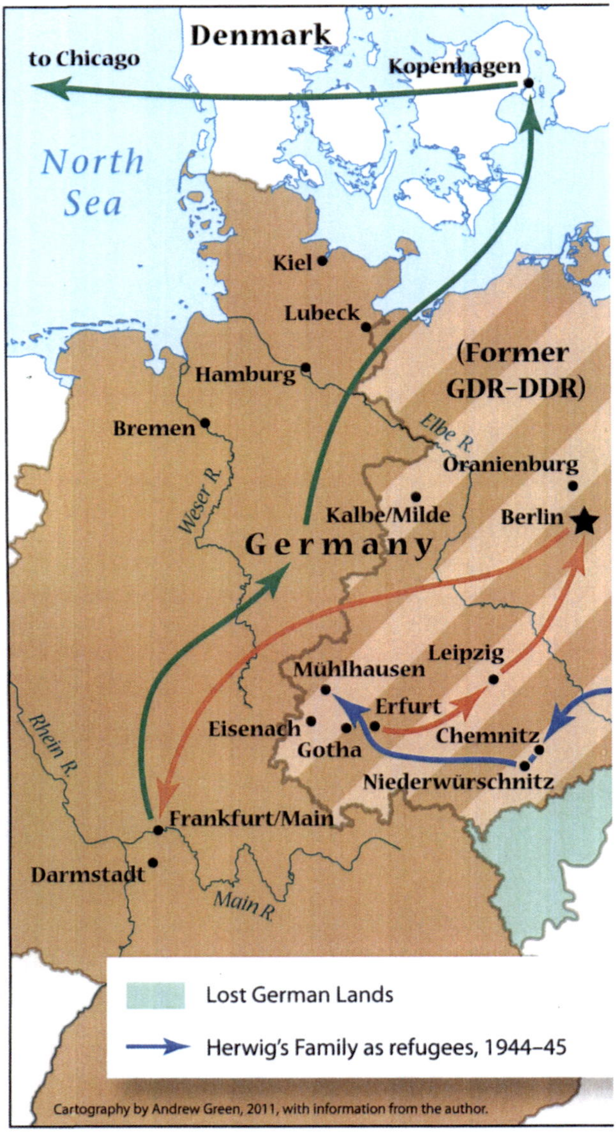
Denmark
to Chicago
Kopenhagen
North Sea
Kiel
Lubeck
(Former GDR-DDR)
Hamburg
Bremen
Elbe R.
Oranienburg
Weser R.
Kalbe/Milde
Berlin
Germany
Leipzig
Mühlhausen
Erfurt
Eisenach
Chemnitz
Gotha
Rhein R.
Niederwürschnitz
Frankfurt/Main
Darmstadt
Main R.
Lost German Lands
Herwig's Family as refugees, 1944–45
Cartography by Andrew Green, 2011, with information from the author.

Sweden
Baltic Sea
Memel
(Klaipeda)
Heydekrug (Silute)
Memel R.
Tilsit
Königsberg
(Kaliningrad)
Danzig
Elbing
Ost
Preussen
Stettin
(Szczecin)
Pommern
Oder R.
Torun (Thorn)
Poznan (Posen)
Poland
0 50 100 miles
0 50 100 kilometers
Neisse R.
Glogau
Schlesien
Breslau (Wrozlav)
Brieg (Brzeg)
Sudetenland
Prague
Political Germany
1926–2011
important stations
in Herwig's life
Herwig & Wolfgang escape
from Communism, 1955
Herwig & Heidi to USA, 1960

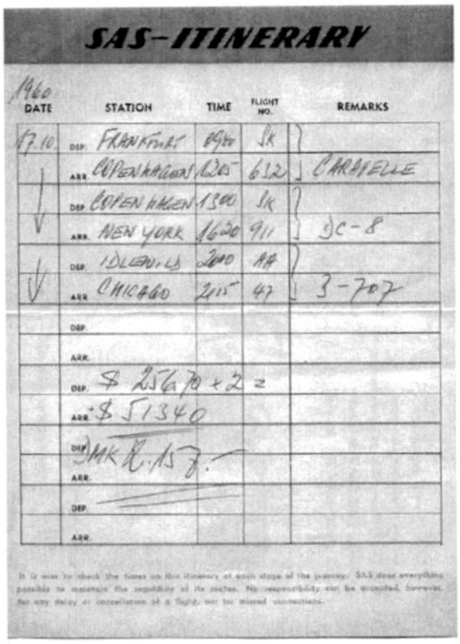

suit, who must have watched these young people looking bewildered. He looked at our tickets and then directed us to a proper gate for a flight to Chicago.

Eckart (Ike) Leistikow, our Chicago contact person from Rand McNally, was waiting for us. Flight after flight from New York brought no Schutzlers. What was a man to do but drink some beer and wait, and that he did. He was there for us as we finally arrived. On our way to a hotel in Evanston, we stopped at a bar with the name of "The Flame" in order to toast to our arrival in the United States of America.

Our hotel in Evanston was an apartment hotel that included a small kitchen. This way we could eat in and save money. We bought a tin of coffee, some bread that was too soft for us, and a package of butter. There we learned that Americans eat salted butter on sandwiches, including under marmalade. That evening, we walked to the shore of Lake Michigan and we thought we stood at the edge of the ocean. We could not believe that this was called a lake but was actually a sea. We then met Ike's wife Lieselotte ("Lisa" or "Lotti") and their very young, two-week-old daughter Karin (nicknamed "Chippy").

On Monday morning I went to Rand McNally in Skokie (a suburb of Chicago) to present myself to the management and look at my new workplace. Everything was of course so very different from what we had been used to in Germany, so I was very apprehensive. What hit me this first day was that the man who had arranged my being there was leaving the company that very day. So from now on, Ike was put in charge of interpreting for me. There was an awful lot to learn, besides the language. The film and photo section was located next to the cartography section and the people working there belonged to a union. I did not know about these strange separations of work between non-union and union workers in the U.S.A. One day I worked on a piece of print film, correcting a mistake I had noticed. I thought I saved somebody some time. That action almost caused a walkout by union members. Non-union people do not touch union work! Live and learn.

After a few days at the hotel, we moved out and in the excitement forgot the tin of coffee. That hurt, considering the financial status we were living under. We had rented a small, furnished apartment on the far north side of Chicago, almost in Evanston on Paulina Street. It included a small living room, a kitchen, a walk-in closet and the bedroom was so small we had to climb over the bed (a metal unit) in order to open or close the window.

The custodians of the building were from Germany; they said some 30 years, but their German language was quite a mixture of both languages—whatever word came first to mind or an aberration of it. We needed everything from pots to pans. We found out that we were renting in what was back then a very Jewish neighborhood. There was a hardware store nearby and we went there to buy a few things. That storeowner quickly understood where we had come from and must have made a few dollars of extra profit on us.

We bought a television set, in order to see and hear the news and get familiar with the sound of the English language. Every morning I bought a newspaper and looked at the pictures and the captions, having a dictionary next to me. I was able to do my work within a year's time without an interpreter. Heidi had arranged in the meantime to baby-sit for Lotti's daughter and we would spend the evenings there. Heidi was working at Rand McNally in the compilation department. She was paid $1.65 per hour and I got $2.20 per hour. We had to pay off $600 for the airfare to America.

Ike arranged for us to meet a few people. They took us under their wings and gave us all sorts of household items such as an ironing board and an iron, etc. He also arranged to open a credit line at a German furniture store in the German neighborhood. We bought a couch table, a lamp and a chair. We still have the table and the chair today.

We were thinking of having a child, therefore we needed a larger place. We found another apartment on North Birchwood Avenue in the Rogers Park area, about two blocks south of our first apartment. On the third floor, under the flat roof, we rented a large living room, a bedroom with a sun porch, a large dining room, and an eat-in kitchen. We had the landlord put in a temporary wall in the dining room, to create a bedroom for the upcoming child. The back windows looked at a brick wall, from the front windows we could see a large intersection and could see and hear the famous Chicago elevated train, and on winter days we could see Lake Michigan looking left out of the window.

The landlady, Linda, would say, "Kids, you need air-conditioning," and we would say, "No way, we love the heat, it's great to be warm." We had come from central Europe and our bodies were starved for sunshine. Well, by the second summer we started to install window air conditioning units in the bedrooms!

Another major event in our life was happening. Mike was born on January 6, 1962, during a roaring blizzard after three days of very hard labor for Heidi. It was at the Evanston Hospital. We both really wanted a child and had hoped for a boy. That wish was fulfilled.

Heidi's job at Rand McNally was now over, because we had paid off the money advance and back in those years companies did not favor for husbands and wives to work in the same place. Besides, now we had a baby to care for. Money was very tight or better said, not in existence. Heidi got a part-time job at Wieboldt's Department Store in Evanston selling lady's hats and teaching ladies how to knit. She did that in the evening, after I got home, and I would stay with Mike.

We shopped only for what was needed for Mike and for us and since Heidi stayed home with Mike, she prepared all the meals and I packed a lunch. She also prepared most of the baby food, from scratch. It was more affordable that way. Going out to eat was out of the question. Also, I got home very late a lot of times and Heidi and Mike had eaten by then.

We were missing the taste of German rye bread and we heard that there was a Jewish bakery that sold that type of bread. One day I walked into the store and asked in my very heavy accented language for rye "*brett.*" The storekeeper looked at me in some strange way and then walked to the back of the store. I thought he was looking for rye bread, although I could see it right in front of me. Nothing happened. The store door opened and another customer walks in and is asking for some things. The man appeared from the rear of the store and served this new customer, ignoring me. So I repeated my wish and was ignored again. I walked back to the apartment and asked my landlord what to do about this situation. He laughed and said, "He is Jewish and he knows you are German. He does not like Germans, keep trying." And so I did. I went back and stated my wish, the baker than asked, "Do you have money, to pay for the bread?" Well, we came to an understanding and from then on we had rye bread.

Our neighbor across the hall was also Jewish and when we would pass on the stairs we would say either hello or good evening or whatever was appropriate for the time of the day. He would totally ignore us and say nothing in reply. After a while I would again ask the landlord what to do. He said the neighbor has a message for me: "Tell this German to learn to speak English, then I will answer him." I think I must have learned to speak the language OK for his approval, because years later after we had become good friends with him, he invited Heidi and I to the wedding of his older daughter. We were the only gentile couple at that wedding in Lincolnwood. I also helped him to the hospital during a heart attack! Good thing he accepted us, or he might have died!

Money or the lack of it was still a very big problem in our household. There was one thing that helped us. We found out that it was not necessary to buy light bulbs. All one had to do was pay the monthly electric bill at the local power company store and they would in turn give you all the light bulbs that you needed, free! Also, cooking gas was free. No charge!

Professionally I did quite well at Rand McNally. Within two years I became lead cartographer, teaching a bunch of much older cartographers the latest ways of drafting called "scribing," an engraving process, and I was put in charge of map drafting for a large educational publisher.

In the meantime Heidi was pregnant again. We wanted Mike to have a playmate and again we had hoped it to be a boy. Peter was born on March 20, 1965, in the hospital at Arlington Heights. It was arranged by fate that there was a blizzard on that day, just as it had been during Mike's birth! Well, now we were four people. I needed to make some financial moves, in order to improve our financial woes.

Ike, his father Leo, one of our colleagues at Rand McNally, and I started to lay plans for forming a cartographic firm of our own. A lot of planning, but mostly talking was going on between us. Ike had drawn up a plan of the "organization," for instance a person who would be president and treasurer and product planner, etc. There was another colleague, who wanted to be "on the ground floor" of this new organization but was not invited, and he blew the whistle to the corporation's management.

On one Friday afternoon Ike, Joe and I were fired from our jobs. We went to a bar next door to have a beer and discuss what we were to do next. I called Heidi and informed her about the firing. When I got home, Heidi had prepared a very nice dinner as a celebration of the start of a "new career"—whatever that was going to be. Yes, we had ideas about forming a company, but there was nothing concrete in existence, just our ideas! I needed a job fast.

So, I started to read the job openings in the paper and saw the advertisement for a map draftsman. When I called, the Chicago Police Department answered. Lo and behold, two weeks later I started to work downtown at the police headquarters. They needed well drawn "beat maps" within the districts and what they had at the time was very inadequate. They were very impressed with my work. These maps were used by the officers in their squad cars within the "beat" of their patrol. We also updated the console maps used by the dispatchers in their work of dispatching officers to trouble spots within the city. There were 27 districts within the City of Chicago. Each dispatcher sat in front of a large, backlighted console showing the district and the "beats" within. It was very interesting work

Young Herwig among his colleagues at the Graphic Arts Section, Chicago Police Department.

and I met some very nice people and got a very good look into the workings of a major police force.

The trouble was, the pay was not enough to cover all the expenses Heidi and I had. So I got one additional job at Western Electric Company of Chicago. They needed to convert electric circuit drawings drawn on paper that had been glued to cloth. We had to transfer this onto a film-like material, similar to Mylar. The company had hired a lot of people just like me, who would do that task on a part-time basis. I left my job at police headquarters at 4:30 and bus over to the west side, punch a clock and sit down and draw lines and strange-looking codes until midnight. Then I took the elevated train back home, go to bed and start the same thing the next morning. At least the money started to improve.

The relationship with our landlord on Birchwood was very interesting. Linda was the landlady and she had become Heidi's friend. Her soft demeanor and availabilities to Heidi's needs were of great help to us. She was in charge of six children, three from her husband's first marriage and three of her own. When Heidi needed somebody to talk to, Linda would be there. She was a very good soul. Then there was the mother of her husband. She was known as "Granny." She was a very small person, but boy, was she a pistol! Her son was her baby and she would do anything for him and nothing for her daughter-in-Law. He was the landlord, and a somewhat dubious member of the Chicago Police Department. One day he said to me, "I love to collect money," and he reached into his trouser pocket and produced a roll of banknotes, hundreds and fifties. He also taught me how to drive a car. He had a big, stick shift Pontiac and told me I will pass his test when we no longer hear the keys jingle in the ignition as I shifted. I learned how to do that well enough to pass my driver's test at the state testing grounds.

The first car we bought was a 1953 Chevy Bel Air. A fellow cartographer sold it to me for $50.00. It had a matte mustard color and I decided to repaint it myself! Ike Leistikow allowed me to use his driveway and his electric sander. After sanding and patching, I taped over all non-paintable surfaces and then proceeded to spray paint it turquoise! We had a new car!

During this time, we started slowly to build a map company. We all had regular jobs, so the founding work had to be done on weekends. Needless to say, I saw very little of my family at that time. We had rented a store on Catalpa Street on the north side of Chicago and started to renovate it into offices and a map photo laboratory. Ike and his father tried to find map publishers interested in professional cartographic work.

Universal Map, Inc., was finally founded. I had established a very good relationship with the educational publisher Scott Foresman in Glenview, Ill. They became one of our first customers. As that endeavor took a good step forward, I could cut down on my other jobs and within a year and a half after leaving Rand McNally we made a profit.

Ike and his father Leo decided to sell this very young company to a manufacturer of industrial ventilation products in Wheeling, Ill. We were given some very nice quarters within their complex. Things looked great! We all had very nice titles; I was Vice President for Map Production and also had some sales responsibilities. But everyone also worked over the light tables and very long hours. I only went home to wash, sleep and go back to work. Sometimes, this went on for many weeks. In normal weather it would take me about an hour and a half to get to work. This was very different in the wintertime when that time could be two and a half to three hours. When I got to our apartment building, there were no parking spaces. I would drive in larger and larger circles until I found a spot. If the temperature was under minus 15 degrees, I took the car battery out and carried it home. This assured me that the car would start in the morning. Another trick I learned to start a "dead" car was to take the cover off the carburetor, move the butterfly of the carburetor with a finger and then add a few drops of rubbing alcohol over the butterfly and turn the key. Most times it worked!

These first years of our life and marriage were not easy in many ways. Having no extra money for anything unforeseen was one problem. We had two children. Heidi had no help and I worked ridiculous hours. We had one car that I drove to work. Whenever Heidi needed to see a doctor for the kids, she had to bundle them up and walk to the office. Holding one child in her arms and the other holding her hand was not an easy thing in Chicago in the wintertime. Heidi lived like on an island. Sure we had tension—and no place to run to! When I wanted to relax and drank too much, that made matters worse at times. Well, we stayed together and grew together! We managed as best as we could, buying only what was absolutely necessary. Food was measured, eggs we bought perhaps six at the time. Going out to eat was not in the cards. A special treat we gave ourselves around Christmastime was to eat at the International House of Pancakes!

We started to get road map contract work from R.R. Donnelley. They had just started, under the direction of Duncan Fitchet, to get into the mapping business and had laid out a very extensive program. One day I had just signed a new contract with Scott Foresman and entered the office in a happy mood, only to be told that our "parent" company was closing us down. As we learned pretty fast, it was for tax reasons. Ike and Joe joined with R.R. Donnelley.

I was stubborn and did not want to give up this hard established venture. So another cartographer and I rented a small business unit in Palatine, Ill., on the northwest side of Chicago and we founded Uni-Map. We continued and expanded quite nicely. We also continued the work for Donnelley. One day

Duncan asked me to take on one young man for a few weeks to let him understand and learn how maps are done. He had just hired this man right out of the U.S. Navy to become a map salesman. This man had wonderful credentials and also had a good pedigree. He became Duncan's protégé and eventual successor.

The man turned out to be a fast learner and was eager to please everybody. I remember dropping him off at the elevated station. He also started on the bottom, so to speak. I remember when he told me about the used car he had just purchased. He also had started to date a very nice young lady. My daily travel to Palatine usually took about the same amount of time as before, so the commute was not easy! I also did some freelance airbrush artwork for Duncan's Lake Winnipesaukee Map and also the very large U.S. Map, which became the master terrain base for a large number of maps for Donnelley, the National Park Service, GeoSystems and MapQuest in later years.

This large work, at the scale of 1:7.5 million is now in my possession, awaiting a donation to the Maps and Geography Division at the Library of Congress, together with some of my other works.

In the early summer of 1968, we were vacationing in southern Illinois on a long weekend and were swimming in a hotel pool when Heidi discovered a very visible swelling in her abdomen. We broke off the easy time and headed home to see a doctor. After an examination, it was determined that there was an ovarian cyst that needed an immediate operation. It turned out to be a benign 5 lb. ovarian cyst.

On the day of Heidi's admittance to the hospital, I found a letter from the Metropolitan Life Ins. Co., telling me that

This was some airbrush test work I did in 1968.

Herwig with his 7.5 million scale art, 2010.

they cancelled my policy because we had allegedly withheld medical information about Heidi's cyst. They also returned the money I had paid into the policy. It was panic time! I was livid. We had no prior knowledge of a cyst. The lawyer said we could fight it, but we would have to carry all the costs getting there. Of course we had no money for that kind of legal battle. As a matter of fact, I had to pay the hospital fee, the surgeon fee and the anesthesiologist fee out of my pocket and needed money fast. I found a Chicago area loan shark that gave me the cash with some horrendous interest. One time I was late with the payment and Heidi got a threatening phone call. We paid that off as fast as we could!

Duncan made the next move and started to invite me to his house to ask me to come join him, Ike and Joe at Donnelley. I really did not want to do that, enjoying the freedom of independence. But Duncan persisted and told me that I needed to give my family better, more stable security by joining a large organization. He had big plans for the future and he said he needed me to help achieve these plans. On September 1, 1967, I became a member of the R.R. Donnelley & Sons, Co., and moved into an office in Northbrook, Ill. My starting pay was $1017.00 per month and it was raised to $1067.00 on May 1, 1968!

CHAPTER 9

My Years With R.R. Donnelley & Sons, Co.

Duncan started to lay plans to establish R.R. Donnelley as a major mapmaking firm within the U.S. I started to travel to various states in the Midwest, in order to establish contacts within the State Departments of Transportation. This was needed to update the Donnelley map program. I often took Heidi and the boys along. They would sightsee or wait for me and we did this together. This way we got to see parts of our country that were still unknown to us and we could be together. We also helped Duncan in the search for the site for the new mapping division organization. It was decided to do this in Lancaster, Pa. Donnelley already had a printing facility there and some of the road maps were being printed and folded there. The location was close to New York City and Washington, D.C. Both cities had many publishers and D.C. had the Library of Congress to which we needed access.

It was 1969 and Heidi and I discussed the possible move for us. We had friends in Chicago and we felt comfortable there. Some people even made some job offers to me, including becoming a maitre d' in a German restaurant controlled by the mafia. Oh well, off we went to the Amish country instead. I thought at the time that we would live in Lancaster for only a few years. How wrong I was. The company sent me to Lancaster to look for an apartment. It was evening when I arrived there and I needed a taxi to take me to a hotel. There were no taxis at the airport. So a taxi had to be called from the city and that took some time. The airport manager came to me and said, "You are the last person here. When your taxi arrives, would you be so kind and lock up the front door? Here is the key. When the door is locked, please place the key over the door frame on that little ledge." That was Lancaster when life was much simpler!

We rented a simple but very nice apartment in the Sweetbriar Complex on the Oregon Pike. Boy, how my life had improved since 1955! There was a swimming pool available and that was used to its full capacity by Heidi and Mike and a little bit more reluctantly by Peter and very little by me. I would only immerse my body up to my armpits, for I was not a swimmer . . . yet. I had very serious ear problems since my early childhood and in the course of many bad ear infections had lost the eardrum in my right ear. In addition, all the inner ear structures of the so-called "small bones" had been eaten away by these infections. My left ear was in a little better shape. There I had half of an eardrum, but also no inner bones. All my life I have had to be careful to not get any water into my ears. Soon, I would learn to be more comfortable in the water!

Ike, Joe Schilacci, a man named Ray Druce, and I in the meantime built up a cartographic operation for Donnelley under Duncan's direction. We rented two floors of an old Victorian mansion in Lancaster on Duke Street. Duncan had his office in Chicago and would visit us 2-3 days per week. Poor Joe had developed incurable leukemia within the last few years and died the first year we were in Lancaster. Luis Freile, the former Map Librarian of Rand McNally, joined our operation one month after my start. He was charged with building up a map library for us. He did that very well. Over the years it was known as one of the top map libraries in the Mid Atlantic Region. We had hired a number of people from the local area and also from a local university. Duncan and the other sales people worked out of the Chicago area.

Duncan set up some very tough rules and he had very high expectations as to our various duties. His first rule was "No Failing." If one of us failed, he and the rest of us together would taste the wrath of Duncan. There were very long hours of hard work. We all reacted in our own way to that. Some of us swallowed it and became physically sick from it. Some never gave up trying to please the man, to the point of giving up all personal pride. I for one swore, "I will outlive the bastard!" Ultimately, I did. Although, in retrospect, I must admit Duncan's tough rules made us all very disciplined and had shaped us into a very professional group.

Heidi and I had purchased a very large camping tent that could sleep eight people and we started to go camping. It was fun and cut down on expenses. We went to the Poconos near Bushkill Falls. On that trip we purchased the Prussian cavalry leather helmet in our possession today. We went to the shore, to the Carolinas, etc. We fished, swam, made campfires and generally had a good time. On a visit to Myrtle Beach, Mike had gone out a little bit too far on a raft and could not make it back on his own. A lifeguard brought him back and our nerves were rattled. That day Heidi decided to learn all about water safety. Through this she started on the path of what would become a long and involved career in aquatics. She received her Water Safety Instructor Certificate and started to work at Golden Meadows Swim Center in Lancaster in 1972. She became a coach and worked with all the major swim clubs in the county as a swim coach for 25 years. Mike, of course, in the meantime had become a competitive swimmer. Heidi, the coach, and Mike, accompanied by Peter and I went to swim meets all over the Mid Atlantic Region. When Peter came of age, he decided to follow in his brother's footsteps. Heidi coached for 25 years and then concentrated on water safety and aquatic exercise programs through the American Red Cross. She became an Instructor-Trainer for the general lifeguard and water safety programs. Wow, what a career Mike's near drowning had started!

One day I got a phone call from my father's wife Marie in Kalbe/Milde, East Germany. My father had died on January 27, 1971. He is now buried in that town; perhaps one day I might be able to visit.

In 1972 we thought we would go to Germany for a visit and look around to see if we could move back. I looked at a few companies, did some talking and listening. One day I came back from one of these fact-gathering trips and Heidi and I looked at each other and we decided that we did not fit into the German lifestyle anymore. Heidi said, "Let's go back and buy a house and settle in!"

At first I had stayed by invitation at Heidi's mother's apartment. One evening she started to become her old self again and said some very unpleasant things to me. I guess she was sensing that we had made up our minds to stay in the U.S. That night I moved into my brother's apartment to avoid ugly scenes with Heidi's mother in front of our children. On the last night in Frankfurt, my brother took us all for dinner at a restaurant. Wolfgang's daughter Angela was there and so was his son Roland. Then we all went to sleep to rest up for the journey on the following morning.

I woke up in the middle of the night, feeling an oncoming fever. I got sicker by the minute and by the morning was already half delirious. A doctor was called and upon his visit decided to put me into a hospital. Not too far from my brother's place was a just completed, modern trauma center. It was discovered that I had a very bad case of staph infection. This was caused by a scrape I had on my left elbow. My arm swelled up and turned to an angry red color. Most of the time I was not conscious and had a lot of pain. I was given massive doses of penicillin and other medications. Then the doctors talked to my family and told them it would be best for my survival, if they would amputate the arm. This sounded too radical to some and especially Heidi. So it was then agreed to wait another day. I must have worsened, because they wheeled me out of the room. I was moved into a hall and they parked the gurney behind a curtain. I woke up in the meantime and was wondering if anybody knew that I was about to die. Well, very obviously I did not die. My body had fought off the bacteria and the fever broke. I must have looked like hell and the arm became a point of interest, since quite a few doctors showed up to have a look at it. They even took photographs of it.

This now turned into a long road to recovery. It was discovered that I was allergic to penicillin. I had developed a rash all over my body and was rapidly losing the skin off my hands and feet! It came off in large pieces. One day the hospital informed Heidi they needed to see money since I was not on any insurance plan. So Heidi called my boss at R.R. Donnelley and he advanced money out of his own personal funds. That was a big help and a load off our minds. For three weeks they continued to treat me. Heidi was back in the States, because our apartment lease ran out, and she had to find a place for us to live.

After another three weeks, a lot of pain and very little improvement, I asked to be discharged. After signing the necessary forms relieving the hospital of any responsibilities regarding my health, they put my arm into a cast. The next day I was on a plane flying home. After a visit at my doctor in Lancaster and receiving some very fine antibiotics, I was back on the mend within days! Thank God for the miracle of modern American medicine. Heidi and I now could concentrate on building and buying a house!

We had very little money. Lancaster was at the start of a population growth that has not eased, even to this day. Builders put up "spec houses" or houses where not enough buyers were available. We found a builder who was developing very nice houses on the NW side of Lancaster. We told them we had $2,000 in cash and I had a solid job. What could be done? They said if we do the painting of all the woodwork, inside and outside, they would take that labor cost and put it up as cash from us toward the down payment. Well, that was a great deal and all four of us started to paint. We also let the entire downstairs remain unfinished. We would work at that little by little ourselves over the next few years. We were the fourth house on Surrey Drive and Candlewyk Drive!

Donnelley started to become established as a strong competitor to Rand McNally and other well-known mapmakers in the United States. I was appointed Supervisor for the development of educational maps. In that capacity I started to meet more and more publishing editors at various publishing houses in the United States. My motto had always been: "*Be helpful and respond quickly.*" That was appreciated and resulted in a very fine relationship with these people and also helped us to create a very nice list of customers.

One of our big supporters at Donnelley turned out to be Mr. James R. Donnelley. He loved maps and cartographers and was a very hard worker in the company. He was also a supporter of me personally and always made sure to see me and say hello whenever he came on business to Lancaster. His first wife was German, which might have helped!

The History and the Process of *Mapmaking*

I think it is important for me to go over the history and process of mapmaking. Mapmaking goes back to the Sumerians! We cartographers call ourselves the second oldest profession! In the time of the ancient Sumerians the kings needed wealth and so they taxed the people. One good source was the real estate tax. So, they surveyed the landholders' estates and figured out a monetary value of that land. Then a tax was figured out, not very much different from how it is done today.

These surveys were inscribed into clay tablets, and voilà, you have the first map! Entrepreneurial people created intercontinental commerce via horses, mules, camels and oxen. They had scribes with them that had to take notes of the surrounding landscape, which is what we now call geography. Then came the period of ocean discoveries. Islands, seashores and harbors were meticulously sketched and then drawn and painted onto vellums and quality papers. Incidentally, these particular map's in the years between the 1400s and the 1700s were treated as state property. If you would smuggle them into the hands of another country and get caught you could face execution for treason. Just think of all the gold and silver that came from the Americas and you will understand why that was so.

The next step was to engrave these features into copperplate in order to print more copies of the same. Then the lithographic process was developed in 1796 in Germany. At first images were created in reverse (mirror copy) on highly polished limestone surfaces using oil-based inks (China ink). The surface was then treated with chemicals that made the drawn image accept ink while the rest of the surface would reject ink. In later years the stone was retired and the zinc plate took its place for many years.

I myself learned to draw on lithographic stones in Mühlhausen, Germany, drawing images of bottle labels. Therefore I

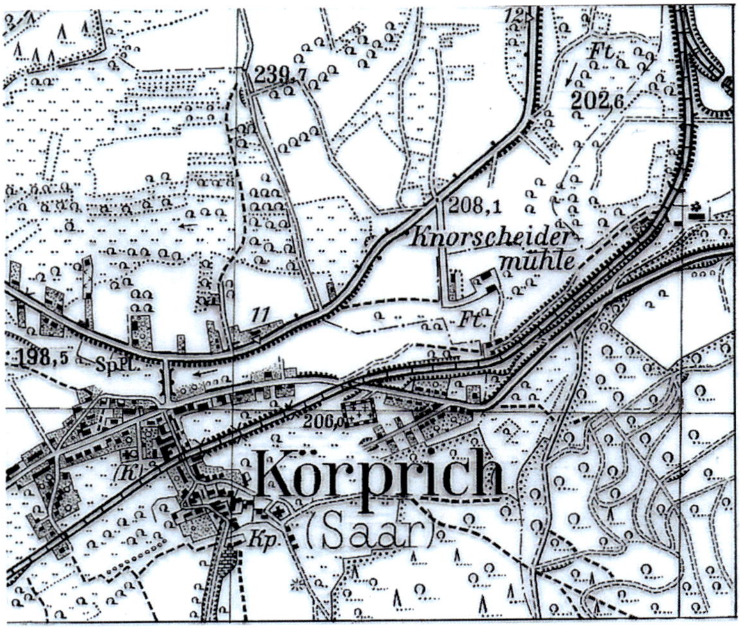

Hand-drawn map by Herwig Schutzler, November 1955, part of my final exam graduating as cartographer in Frankfurt/Main. Every line, every symbol and every line of type you see above has been drawn by hand! As a matter of fact, both Heidi and I, when we were students of cartography, had to learn how to construct and draw any font of type, in many sizes, on various media for one year!

can honestly claim that *I have come out of the stone age of drafting!* The drafting process was to draw with ink on cloth at first, followed by inking on specially prepared papers. Zinc plates that were treated with a coat of chalk (calcium carbonate) and that coat was then hardened, took the place of the heavy, cumbersome stones.

In the late 1950s the engraving was on coated glass plates. This was developed in Switzerland and was the newest way of drafting. That is what I learned to do at the Institut in Frank-

Here you see a map drawn by hand by Heidi in her first year of apprenticeship at the Institut in 1956.

furt/Main. I took that process to the U.S.A. where we engraved the images onto coated Mylar sheets. All map type was applied word by word individually.

Curved type, such as along rivers, were done letter by letter. In the old ink days, we would letter all type letter by letter, in all necessary sizes as prescribed. We used to call this "brain surgeon" work. In the Institut in Frankfurt I was schooled in the techniques of geographic relief drawings, following the ideas of Prof. Imhoff in Switzerland. One had to have graphic and artistic understandings of light and shade, just like a fine artist. In addition, one had to have enough geographic understanding of the geomorphology of the Earth. This helped me in later years in the U.S.A. to earn money to feed my family.

All this was explaining the drafting processes. Cartography, of course, is the science that explains and teaches the ability to create flat images of the round Earth onto printable surfaces. In order to do that, projections had to be developed that would enable us to do so. Geometry and mathematics, together with the understanding of the true shape of the planet are the main ingredients. A simple example of this is the peeling of an orange. You then lay these peels across a flat surface and mathematically and geometrically you expand the upper and lower peel section, until the voids fill in between. Of course there are many such projections being used for different map purposes.

Surveyors and geodesists used to go out into the field and with triangulations mapped the visible geography onto paper. These notes were then given to a cartographer, who would precisely, using agreed symbolizations and graphics, "portray" the measured geography onto the projected surface.

During and after WWI and through WWII aerial photography was developed, refined and triangulations were incorporated into stereo-planigraphic machines. Dual pictures, a few degrees apart, would be taken and then loaded into the machines and the operator then applied the mechanics of the machine, together with his ability to read the pictures, to "draw" the geography onto paper via a mechanical arm. The image would photographically be transposed onto draftable surfaces such as engraving Mylar as mentioned above.

As the computer was developed and used as a tool, satellite photography, with its computer mechanics, now does the surveying and the cartographic development processes are speeded up immensely. All of this in simple terms explains how I, as a professional cartographer, earned my living. I loved every minute of it.

We worked very hard in those 18 years at 700 North Duke Street. We worked 6 full days per week, plus overtime 3 days of the first 5 days in a week. Through 1972, we supervisors got no overtime pay! Then we found out, that throughout the RRD plants in Lancaster supervisors were entitled to OT pay. We rattled the cage and from then on got paid for our work.

Everyone dreaded Duncan's visits from Chicago. Once in a while, after a very crazy day with everybody jumping to please the master, he would invite us for drinks at his favorite drinking hole—the *Rose Bowl.*

Cartographic engraver, measuring scope and lupe.

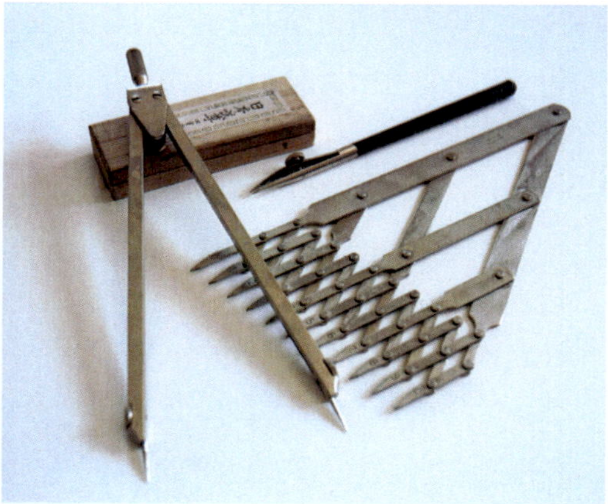

Some pre-computer cartographer tools: China ink, ruling pen, compass and spacing tool.

Then came Christmastime. He invited everyone and their spouses to a party at some nice restaurant in Lancaster. He got to show appreciation to the "gals" for supporting us throughout the year. He then would pick his favorite female for the evening and would give that poor lady all of his attention, including constant invitations to drink.

One afternoon at the office on party day, he had asked me to do quite a big task. I called Heidi and said to lay low, not knowing if I could make it. At 5:30 Duncan was walking out of his office, when he saw me at the light table he said, "What the hell are you doing here? Why are you not picking up Heidi?" I told him I had to finish the task he asked me to do. His response? "To hell with it. There is a f….. Christmas party tonight, to which I have invited everybody and their spouses and you better be there!" From then on we called the annual party the "f……. party." In later years, when Sid became VP, he also invited us, sometimes to his house on Wheatland Avenue. Duncan would then be the guest of honor.

Toward the later 1970s Heidi was asked by friends of ours if she ever considered picking up her singing again. She decided one day to start up again. She participated in the local Kiwanis production of the *King and I* as one of the wives. As fate would have it, our granddaughter Megan in Seattle did her first theater participation in *The King and I* as one of the children at age 9! Heidi spent the next 15 years with the Lancaster Opera Workshop, later known as the Lancaster Opera Company. Her first big role was in *The Tales of Hoffman* as the Magic Doll Olympia. Our sons and I would also participate behind the scenes as helpers/stage crew. We had more time as a family that way. At that time the Lancaster newspapers ran a big article about the "Diving Diva" on the local stage. When Duncan saw the article, he immediately contacted the R.R. Donnelley house publication. We as a family were interviewed and then they ran the major lead article, accompanied by many pictures, in the following month's issue. In 1980 Heidi landed her dream role as the Queen of the Night in Mozart's *The Magic Flute*. This was her greatest achievement. Her voice is just so clear and powerful, there is in my opinion, no equal. For many years and even to this day, people that knew us would compliment Heidi about singing that role.

In 1981 she was Fiordiligi in *Cosi Fan Tute* and her last role on stage was in 1984 as Rosalinde in *Die Fledermaus*. Heidi had developed a lot of pain in her back and could hardly walk. As it turned out, she had a cyst on her spine near the main nerve. That was repaired surgically very successfully in 1985 and she recovered quite nicely. The years at the theater were good for all of us in the family. Mike, Peter and I helped out backstage and we could spend a lot of time together.

Our cartographic unit at R.R. Donnelley had established an early association with a cartographic firm in Vermont, and we pushed a lot of our "grunt" work up there. It required many visits from us to assure that they would work to our standards. At one time I spent all of December and January up there. So after Christmas, I took Heidi and the boys with me for a few days of winter holiday. We played around in the snow and did our first *snowmobiling*. Ed Whelan, the man who ran the company, invited us to dinners, etc. His house was always open to us, literally. At one dinner he had ordered oysters and invited

Mike to try one, he did, but immediately spit it into a napkin! He was eight years old at the time.

Duncan retired and moved to his new house outside of Hanover, NH, and took on a teaching position. He taught a course on the "History of Cartography" at Dartmouth, his alma mater. He also concentrated on the upkeep and publication of his beloved Lake Winnipesaukee Maps. On his last official day as VP he invited Heidi and I for a last dinner in Lancaster at the Greens Restaurant of Overlook Park. Here he announced a very big pay increase to my salary. He actually added that money is more important than titles. He went on to tell me that I would never be a manager at RRD, because I didn't have a degree from a reputable American college or university. Oh well, I thought, we shall see about that.

During this time several things happened both good and bad. Our good friend Ray died of a very rare blood disease, similar to cancer. Ike left to manage the Cartography Division at the Pennsylvania Department of Transportation in Harrisburg. Finally, I was in for a big surprise that proved Duncan wrong—Sid promoted me to Manager of Cartographic Operations!

At one time I attended a manager seminar in Chicago at RRD headquarters. By custom, all of us were invited by Jim Donnelley to a cocktail party. He owns a huge double apartment on the Gold Coast of Chicago on Lake Michigan. After security clearance with a guard, I rode up a private elevator to his floor. I stepped out of the door into a rather large room full of all sorts of RRD upper and lower echelon. Jim sees me, steps over to me, lays his arm around my shoulder and bellows,

"Welcome Herwig, my good friend, let's have a single malt." I saw the look on some people's faces, wondering who I was. Bart Faber, the Senior VP of Donnelley, was there as well.

Then, after Jim had fixed us a drink, he took me by my arm and walked over to the windows looking down at the Outer Drive along Lake Michigan and said to me, "Herwig, you have come a long way since you and Heidi came to Chicago and I am glad you work for Donnelley." He was right! I had come a long way. As I looked down to the street level, my thoughts went back to our early years in Chicago and then back home to Germany—two times a refugee and one time an emigrant. Over the years, I had many similar instances when I met, dined and had drinks with important national and international leaders in our business. And I must say, I was appreciated by our customers and by most people within the Donnelley organization. It is amazing what hard work, a strong will, and a good life partner can accomplish.

CHAPTER 10

Becoming Citizens of the United States of America

In early 1980, Heidi and I decided that it was time to become citizens of the United States. We had waited until that time, because of some legal issues we thought were in our way regarding Heidi's mother and father. Besides, we both felt very strongly that it was time for this step. Our children were born here, we paid taxes, and this country gave us the opportunity to achieve what we could only dream to reach in Germany. Economically, we had solid footing here in Lancaster with R.R. Donnelley and we felt very comfortable in this community. I would think back to how well my brother and I were treated when we were refugees in 1955. Heidi and I had to work very hard in the early years in Chicago, but it was also the American economic system that gave people like us the opportunity to reach for as high as you thought you could.

On November 7, 1980, Heidi and I were sworn in by a local judge in the old Lancaster Courthouse. Afterwards, we had a party at our home on Surrey Drive attended by friends and family and Duncan, who was our Official Immigrant Sponsor in 1960, was the guest of honor. Now I, Herwig Georg Heinrich Schutzler, after years of physical and economic struggles, having been a refugee more than once, was now an American and very proud of it! It was all the more special to have Heidi at my side to do the same thing.

God Bless America

Often Heidi and I did not realize how hard we were working. Yes, we were alone, with no help from extended family. We received no handouts from anybody or any organization—no government plans, no tax breaks—just our own determination and work. And that is the way of free enterprise and human spirit. The enterprising spirit and the wish for accomplishment and inner satisfaction will move most people forward, often against all odds. By giving people things on a platter, without letting them work for it, will take their sense of accomplishment away. Just look at the way a lot of East German people came out of decades of living in a government controlled society, first the Hitler years and then the awful "brainwashing" no free thinking communist era. The State guided the people through all their activities of life, work, health, vacation and association. It will take a long time to eradicate that.

My brother Wolfgang and his wife Gardi divorced. They had two children, Roland born in 1955 and Angela, born in 1960. Gardi remarried in Frankfurt/Main. Wolfgang also remarried. That marriage did not last long but produced a son with the name of Michael, who in the 2000s lives in Frankfurt/Main. I met him once at Wolfgang's funeral. For some reason he is keeping to himself.

Now came another difficult moment in my life. My mother, Magdalena (Markscheit) Schutzler, died on the 28th of June 1982. A mother's death, in my opinion, is one of the most dramatic events in a person's life. It is very hard to take and it sinks in deeper and deeper in the following years. I went to Frankfurt and miracle upon miracle, my sister Traute from Schneeberg, East Germany (now Bad Schlema), was allowed out of their "free" totalitarian regime! So my brother, my sister and I were united for the first time since the early 1950s. What a meeting that was! Wolfgang was living in free market socialist West Germany and I was living in the capitalist United States and my sister was living in communist East Germany.

As it turned out, she had become a believer in that awful system. That included being a member of the Communist Party. Years later, after the collapse of the awful system, she gave her Party pin to me.

Only members of the Party were allowed to wear this pin.

Well, I could understand after a while why that was so. She had risen in status, had become a Party member and they lived in relative comfort, when compared with the rest of the population. We had long discussions into the wee hours of the morning; we slept very little for a few days. One day, we took a steamboat trip down the Rhine River and I remember that very fondly—all of us finally spending time together, in the beautiful scenery of the Rhine River—my sister was a very happy woman at that moment.

My sister Traute often surprised me with the direction she took in life. She loved to read, listen to music on the radio and knit, often all of that at the same time! When she married Harry Reichel and the country turned communist, she joined the Party. That became her life. In retrospect, I now can understand what took place. Harry was a very typical German man, who told his wife what to do, what he needed and what he wanted. He was very dictatorial. The Party on the other hand did the same thing to the people as a whole, as I had experienced myself. Well, how strong are we all to resist? Some do, better than others.

In 1984 our son Mike graduated from Penn State University with a degree in Electrical Engineering and his first job took him to Rochester, NY, working for the Harris Corporation. He worked for a number of years for Harris and in that capacity had to travel to many countries. He apparently developed into a very good business negotiator. Over the years, he became a recognized businessman and lives a great life with his wife Cari, daughter Megan, and son Erik in the Seattle area. Over the years Michael ventured into all sorts of businesses in the role of CEO and also ran his own business, teaching people to become good businessmen.

In this same year, our son Peter Schutzler graduated from high school and entered service in the United States Coast

Guard. He told us that he did not want to go to college. A number of teachers in his high school had convinced him that he was not smart enough to go to college. Little did they know! Peter served four exciting years in the United States Coast Guard, serving in Alaska, Hawaii and New York Harbor. While in New York, the Coast Guard, together with the United States Navy, did drug interdiction out of Key West, Florida. Peter spent some time there, as part of his duty. He was invited to attend officers' school, but declined and decided to study secondary education at Penn State. He was an Assistant Principal at a large middle school in Macungie, PA. Later he became Principal in the Catholic School System of the Allentown Diocese.

As a parent and father, I am very proud of the achievements of both my sons. It's hard enough to raise children and it is very difficult to make sure that children stay on the right path. Heidi and I are indeed blessed.

CHAPTER 11

Years of Changes, Years of Travel

Our little RRD Cartographic Division became more and more important as a leader of American mapmaking. We built a very strong relationship with the National Geographic Society and other private large publishers such as *Reader's Digest*. We had outgrown our office. Sid and I picked an old tobacco warehouse in Lancaster City with about 25,000 sq. feet of space. Together with an architectural firm, we laid out plans to convert that building into a modern mapmaking facility. I oversaw the entire process, which meant that this became the center point of my life for a while. We also applied for federal and state recognition as an historic landmark, requiring attendance at all sorts of meetings. Finally, in January 1987, we moved from Duke Street to James Street after a massive snowstorm. I was given a presidential award from RRD for all my work overseeing the construction of the building.

Around this time, Heidi thought it would be good if I would learn how to swim. I became her student and according to Heidi, I was the most challenging student she ever had. But, it worked. My local ear doctor advised me to use Silly Putty to seal off my ears from water. Today, I am mixing Silly Putty with a Silicone wax, that way it is not so sticky in the ear. I am very grateful to Heidi that she helped me to overcome my fear of the water. Because of her patience and my willingness, I now had the chance to experience the world of snorkeling and what a beautiful world that is! Heidi and I have spent countless hours in the Caribbean waters. I have seen fish in all sizes and colors living in their own world. I have been over corals of indescribable beauty and I have been underwater, looking at a 2,000-foot drop off! And of course it is the world of dolphins and whales!

In 1989, Heidi and I did our first Windjammer trip down in the Lesser Antilles and we were "hooked" by the Caribbean tropics and the thrill of the tall ships. Over the course of six trips, on three different ships, we visited all the islands of this part of the Caribbean. Our favorite ship was the *Mandalay*. In the year 1992 we had Michael (he had just divorced from his first wife) and Peter (was about to be married) with us on the *Mandalay* and we spent New Year's together on Palm Island where we also celebrated Mike's 30th birthday. This was very good for all four of us and as it turned out, was the last time we did such a vacation as a family.

I call myself an optimist and a believer that a person can help his own destiny by being honest and follow moral principles. Do not cheat on yourself and of course not on others. Be fair; do not give favors to others before finding out if they are worth your trust. As far as my religious beliefs are concerned,

I believe in a higher being. I believe in a spirit that brings certain order to all things in the entire, infinite Universe. I call myself more of a Protestant Christian, as compared to being a Catholic or belonging to any of the other split-off sections of Christianity. In my life, I have deeply looked into astronomy as a layperson. There is no *chaos* in the Universe. As we learn little by little how all of our known life is structured and built, we find the same order in the Universe. As one astronomer once said: "The more I have learned about the Universe, the more I started to believe in God."

The Muslims I can't quite understand with their belief that only their religion is the only true one and non-believers should be killed. This is not a religion; it is a dogma. Heidi and I both think highly of the North American Plains Indians' belief in the Great Spirit and in their thinking of being the custodian of all things created in nature. Buddhism in my opinion is very similar that way.

Some people call me a conservative. Well, a liberal in the meaning of the 2000s, I am not. There must be law and order in the land, to be followed equally by all people. Preserve the sovereignty of the nation. Keep illegal people out of the country and if they break the law, deport them. That is the law of this land as it is, yesterday and today. Under that same law Heidi and I entered the country. Preserve our boundaries. Do not go out into foreign lands to fight wars unless we are attacked. Set up true social systems that will help the truly poor, the very sick and the disabled. Allow all religions equally to follow their beliefs, but at the same time, become and behave like a citizen of the United States. Our Government is "by the people and for the people," therefore citizens have responsibilities. Learn the English language; we all did! The churches should pay real estate taxes just like any citizen or organization that owns properties. Perhaps I am more of a true libertarian.

I like good music—classic, country, some pop, even good jazz. I like good food and I like to cook good food. I like good wine (South America, Malbec) and good beer (no American big brands but most imports). My favorite meats are beef, pork, fish and poultry. I do not favor veal, turkey, lamb or shellfish. Although, I do like Maryland crab cakes in Maryland! I like potatoes, vegetables and rice. I like to eat German and Jewish rye bread in all its variations. And I *love* a good butter cream tort baked by Heidi. Some of my favorite dishes include: Beef Roulades, Pork Schnitzel a la Holstein (fried egg on top), roasted goose for Christmas, Cabbage Roulades, Goulash, and a fine beef roast spiked with fresh garlic and marinated in red wine and herbs and olive oil for about 24 hours and then roasted on a rotisserie.

I like to read about the old discoveries. Since I have traveled a lot, whenever I fly by plane I like to look out of the window and try to find out where exactly I might be at that moment. I love to work in the vegetable garden or tend to the flowers. I think I am handy with most tools, except electric things. I like to drive and I am handy with all sorts of passenger cars. One of my favorite pastimes is reading books on Earth sciences, good biographies, or good historical accounts, even of the very past. All of Astronomy is another of my areas of interest.

Technologically speaking, I "grew up" with Apple. Most of it I learned by myself, although I had easy access to help in my company. In later years, especially since I am retired, I take a lot of pictures and some video and handle them on my computer using iPhoto and Adobe Photoshop. Heidi and I traveled extensively. One of my greatest trips with Heidi was down to Patagonia. The geography was plain astounding. I had young Darwin's travel log from 1835 with me, as we followed in his footsteps. It is my custom to take notes every day on my trips. When I get home, I will sit down and write the full story of the trip and enhance that with pictures taken during these trips. Over the years I have filled many ring binders with these writings.

Throughout my life, I enjoyed good health. I had eye problems and ear problems, but nothing ever serious. There were no real overnight stays at the hospital, except the staph infection on my arm in 1973. So we were able to do a good bit of traveling.

On the following pages I have condensed some of our more memorable trips to a travel adventure, to give an idea of what we have seen and what my impressions were at the time.

Musings of a Traveler

Herwig G. Schutzler, retired cartographer, 2010

As I am writing this, I consider myself a very lucky man. Why? For one thing I am now 73 years of age and in fairly good health; that alone is worth a lot. The other thing is that I always wanted to travel and see other lands, meet other people and experience their cultures. I did quite a lot of that, so far.

"The Sea that calls all things unto her calls me, and I must embark."

KAHLIL GIBRAN

"In the past I have visited remote places—Japan, Korea, the Galapagos—partly as a way to visit remote states of mind and remote parts of myself that I wouldn't ordinarily explore."

PICO IYER

(changed a little)

I do remember, as I was 15-16 years of age, sitting in my rented room in the town of Erfurt, Germany, and reading a book about the travels of Sven Hedin (1865-1952, a Swedish geographer/explorer in Central Asia) and my mind would start to wander past this man's travels, picturing myself doing just that. I was in my first year of a four-year program to become a cartographer and one of my most favorite studies was physical geography!

I also read about Stanley and Livingstone in Central Africa and at that time I thought I would like to eat a banana right off a tree if I ever get to where bananas grow. I had my dreams and silent wishes and my daily studies in geography did foster these thoughts a lot. I was born near the NE Baltic Sea and some of my relatives had been fishermen and seafarers. The sea is in my veins. The years between this time and my immigration to the U.S.A. were building years, including the time period that came after that. I ate my first banana (not off a tree yet!) of my life in 1955 in West Berlin, after my brother and I had just escaped from the communists.

The Brandenburg Gate, Berlin (1988)

So I left Germany in 1960 to come to the United States of America. I worked hard, and with Heidi's help we established a family and laid the foundation for a good life. My career helped wet my travel appetite very well. I spent many weeks in Quebec, Canada. I went to Germany, Great Britain, Holland, the Czech Republic, Hungary and Spain. Sometimes I had a chance to invite Heidi along. It is good to have companionship when you travel, especially a person you love. In the meantime, Heidi taught me how to swim—a very important necessity in later travels!

The United States of America

A great deal has been written about our great country and I am not the man to add to that. Only what needs to be said within the framework of this particular writing. But one event concerning the history of this country is very important—the expedition of Louis and Clark—initiated by President Jefferson. These courageous men, aided by the assistance of the Mandan Indian people, opened up, the American West, for better or for worse.

St. Louis

I have traveled a fair distance within the 48 States, having crossed the states in one trip from Boston to Seattle. I have been to Maine, Connecticut, Massachusetts and Cape Cod, New Hampshire and Vermont.

I lived in the Midwest for nine years. I have been to the Mid Atlantic all the way down to Florida, including quality times in the Everglades. The Southwest and the great Indian country were amazing and the Grand Canyon filled me with awe and wonderment. The Northwest with its mountains, rain forests, volcanoes, bays and rugged shores look like new creations. The Rocky Mountains with all its splendors and of course Yellowstone. That park alone offers the visitor one of the greatest natural scenes in the world. The geology of the park will get you close to the first days of life on earth and the current botany will let you appreciate nature at its best now.

Travel is Fatal to Prejudice, Bigotry and Narrow-mindedness

The people I met were very interesting. These included the free-thinking New Englanders with their own strong English-colored accent, to the friendly Midwestern people who will make you a cup of coffee any time of the day. The open hospitality of the American West and the reserved Mid Atlantic people, barely give you the time of the day at first but upon getting to know you, will open their hearts. The people of the Old Dominion, they are warm, hospitable and take things at a much slower pace. I have spent time within the land of the original Southwestern people, the Navajo and the Apache. Our land is as big as a continent, is vast, beautiful and also tough. It offers everything a traveler would like to see and feel. Let us hope it will stay that way.

The life near water, in water and on water was always my (our) favorite. I started to look seriously into sailing vacations to other lands. The Barefoot Windjammer Cruises gave us a wonderful start.

Over the Rocky Mountains

These Windjammers make sea travel a real adventure.

A new world opened up for us, place names now became connected with real places and people and events.

Travels to The British Virgin Islands, St. Martin, St. Bartolome, St. Kitts/Nevis, Antigua, Guadeloupe, Dominica, Martinique, St. Lucia, St. Vincent and Grenada

Over the next six sailing voyages, spread out over a number of years, we landed on all of the above islands and many in between. Our taxi took us to the pier for the eventual transfer to our first sailing vessel. We saw the great *Polynesia*, a four-masted barquentine (the name of this type ship originates to the old sailing days, when they were also called barques) anchored off shore. A crew member motoring a small, diesel-powered craft picked us up and my emotions were just impossible to measure. I was in the Caribbean and I was going on a sailing adventure! The year was 1991, 39 years had elapsed from my old dreams and I was breathing tropical air, smelling tropical aromas and enjoying the afternoon sunlight reflecting on the surface of the ocean. Listening to the singsong language of the Creole people became one of the things I would always look forward to. Oh, and listening for the first time to the sound of steel drum music. It has a character of its own and it can't be appreciated away from the Caribbean. The beat and the metal sound have to go under the skin, and combined with the sometimes "smoky" voices of the singers all under the starry night sky, will make you feel like you are in another world.

The crew raised the main sails and some of us would jump in and help pull the heavy lines, while the tune of *Amazing Grace* playing over the on-board sound system made you really feel like you were aboard an old sailing vessel. On and on we would sail—to another island, another port, meeting other people. We would dive into the sea to snorkel between the coral and the tropical fish, accepting the wonders of nature as a gift.

While in Antigua, I would wander among the preserved old shipping installations of Admiral Nelson's fleet and my thoughts went back to the glory days of the British Navy; the greatest navy that ever ruled the world's oceans. I thought about the battles they fought right here in the Caribbean with the French and the Dutch Navies and of course with the pirates. Oh, what privileges I had to experience all of that. Today, Antigua is one of the main starting points and finishing points for sailing people from all over the globe. We met people from Norway, Sweden, Germany, Britain, France, and Australia, some of them in larger vessels, some 50 ft. or 60 ft. Some were in groups and quite a lot of single-handed sailors as well. These were true adventurers, who sail around the world and stop wherever they like and for however long they want to stay.

Ah, Dominica—what memories. This island has the only Indian Territory of all of the Lesser Antilles for the Carib Indians. They try to work out a meager living, depending almost solely on tourists buying baskets or woodcarvings. Here on one of our land trips our driver, using his machete, cut off a bunch of bananas and *I ate my first banana off a tree!* Unfortunately, there is another smell on these islands, different from the aromas of the tropics. The open sewers in the streets of towns and villages, is all part of the daily life.

The French parts of this including Guadeloupe, Martinique and Isle de Saints are just another jewel in these parts. The geography is breathtakingly steep, volcanic mountains, covered in lush greens of various shades of colors. The islands are almost swimming in the turquoise or blue sea and the snow white tufts of clouds topping the peaks.

The SV Mandalay *off Palm Island, Grenadines.*

Take some light provisions and snorkeling gear, hire a boat, and have yourself dropped off on an uninhabited beach to spend hours with the sea, sand, wind and sea life, or just lay there and dream. God, thank you for these moments of living.

Saint Lucia—what a dream world it still was in the early 1990s. The two Pitons! Grande Piton and Petit Piton and in between Soufriere, the volcano one can *drive into*! The snorkeling at the Pitons' drop-off is another dream world of the sea. Grenada and the Grenadines—a world of its own within the Caribbean realm. Grenada, the "American Spice Island" is a true representation of the physical and human geography of this region. It is a very friendly, easygoing population living within their tropical world with all its wonders and trials. There are mountains, waterfalls, silent jungle-like scenes, plantations and vistas that carve themselves vividly into one's memory. There are also the remnants of destructions of mighty hurricanes that visit this and the other islands every so often. After all, the Lesser Antilles are right in the paths of the incoming hurricanes from across the Atlantic.

And the people still smile and most of them lead a very simple life. One time I asked a driver to get me to a shop, because I needed film for my camera. He shouted across the street, "One time Jonathan, my mon here needs some filem, where can he get it? OK, one time, I will get the mon there, so he can buy the filem." I asked, "How do you celebrate Christmas?" "Well, I paint the window frames of the house and we buy some new pillow cases for the beds, no we do not have a Christmas tree, too expensive. Life is simple."

Looking Into the Eye of a Whale

Learning how to swim and snorkel was one of the most important factors in my next sea adventures. We had gone on a wild Atlantic Spotted Dolphin swim in the Atlantic off the shores of Bimini. The idea had been to give my wife a therapeutic cleaning of her body after some major surgery. Schools of the Spotted Atlantic Dolphins gave us company and excitement. These wild and playful creatures of the sea are a pleasure to be with, as long as you do not touch them—one touch and

Eye of a humpback, Silver Banks, NE of Hispaniola. Photo by Joan Andreacchio, and a mutual whale friend.

they swim away. We were on an ocean-going catamaran, about 90 feet in length with two huge diesel engines. This boat would also go in the springtime off the shores of Hispaniola to the Humpback Whale Sanctuary. We, of course, signed up.

In early spring, the North Atlantic Humpback Whale comes down from Norway and Iceland to the Silver Banks coral region about 90 miles offshore of Hispaniola. Our boat would anchor on the reef, near a wrecked cargo ship and we stayed for five days of observing the whales. There they give birth, teach the young ones to swim and breath and mate with the ever-present males.

We did that three times in three different years. I consider these whale swims as one of the most exciting experiences of my life. To be in the water with these very gentle giants and observe them in their habitat and their interactions with each other is one of God's gifts. All major mammal mothers will defend their young ones and move against approaches by humans. Not so the humpback whale. Sometimes you get the feeling that the mother wants to show off their young ones, although they will stay close to protect against any unforeseen events. Many hours just speed by as one floats in the water looking at these wonderful leviathans, and you know that they are also observing you. One time I was about 10 feet away from a resting whale near the water surface and we looked at each other for the longest time . . .

> "If you come to a fork in the road, take it."
>
> YOGI BERRA

Every morning and every afternoon, we would go out, sometimes 4-5 miles away from our "mother ship" and spend time with one of God's greatest creations and watch them interact with each other and with us human beings. One of my favorite moments happened as I floated on the water's surface, supported by my snorkel. About 30 feet below me were two humpbacks, lying next to each other. They either dozed, communicated with each other, or they just watched me. Then they slowly rose to the surface, exchanged air and then dropped back onto the sandy ocean floor.

Europe

I was born in Europe and I love to travel to see as much as I can. When I travel down the Rhine River, I let my mind go back to when this was known as Gaul, the Roman conquests and the emergence of the various Christian Empires. All these people left their mark on the lands, building fortifications and great cities with splendid architecture. The aqueducts, the defensive walls, roads, canals and sprawling vineyards and fields of agriculture are a testimony to the efforts of people throughout the ages. As one travels across these lands, one encounters constant language changes and different dialects within these languages. One encounters various cultural habits and different religions all the time, these being the result of the aforementioned developments of Europe.

I can't help to mention the geography—the rivers both mighty and small, the mountains gentle or ice covered, also swamps, forests and great plains. These great plains of the eastern part of Europe open the paths to great summer heat from the southwest and the cold winter blasts from the east. You can see the flat and below sea level land of Holland and explore the rugged coast of Costa Brava northeast of Barcelona, Spain. There you will experience two totally different zones of geography. You can sit on the banks of the Danube in Budapest and look up at the old city of Buda and its palace and fortifications while you enjoy a glass of dark red Hungarian Bull's Blood. You can walk the very old medieval streets of Prague and appreciate that during The Second World War, no damage was done to this old European citadel.

In the springtime, it is great to travel through the Bohemian countryside in the Czech Republic among the wide, bright yellow fields of rapeseed and as you go through some small town or village, get invited for an impromptu dance and glass of wine as a newlywed couple celebrates new life. You can travel through the eerily empty farm fields of Eastern Poland, formerly old settled German lands given to Poland after The Second World War. The Poles are still not sure if this is now theirs to keep. You can experience the strange handling of what I consider Russia's greatest capture of The Second World War, the old Prussian Province of East Prussia and its capital Königsberg, now called Kaliningrad. For centuries, the Russians wanted this city and the destruction of Prussia. Now that they have it, they let it sort of fall apart. It is dirty and sustains a lot of war damage (after over 60 years). The buildings from the Stalin era are falling apart and the streets and roads are atrocious. The countryside is almost empty! Go figure . . . the Russians treated this place, my former home, just like a piece of war booty.

The Baltic Republics of Lithuania, Latvia and Estonia are historical lands, settled by Slavic people and Germanic people. Kings and emperors and other powerful people disputed this area for many years. It was carved up, reshaped and people were moved north to south and east to west. In this area the merchants established the Hanseatic League. Here Peter the Great built the great city of St. Petersburg in order to entice the West to assist in making Russia a great nation. In The First World War, these countries again were shoved around and its people were forced to suffer. At the end of The Second World War there was little or no peace for these people until the early 1990s. The people are very hospitable and will invite you into their homes for food and drink. Life in the countryside generally is simple and down to earth. A lot of the agricultural work is still done manually and the earth smells rich and fresh. Great cities like Klaipeda, formerly known as Memel, Riga, and Tallinn were all part of the old Hanseatic League. Now they offer the modern traveler a host of historical sites, great architecture and a life that is very different from the western parts of Europe. Tallinn had no war damage during The Second World War and is a showpiece of medieval architecture rivaling Prague.

Tallinn, Estonia

My North Pacific Odyssey

Our very first ocean cruise took us for three weeks around the northern periphery of the Pacific Ocean. We sailed from Seattle through the Inside Passage, past Juneau and Ketchikan and on to Glacier Bay. The majesty of Alaska left a deep impression on my soul and the mighty actions of the glacier world left me astonished and in awe of our natural wonders.

We sailed through the famous Icy Strait into the stormy Gulf of Alaska and then through the Aleutian Island chain, past Dutch Harbor into the Bering Sea, where we were greeted by another storm lasting almost the entire crossing on the way towards the Kamchatka Peninsula. Then I noticed the very steep and tall cliffs of the Siberian coast. We sailed past the rugged little and large rock towers looming out of the water and the sea pounding it relentlessly. Then we sailed forward to huge towering volcanoes, visible within the coastal mountain chain. We entered the Petropavlovsk Bay through a very nar-

Near Petropavlovsk-Kamchatsky, Russia

Between the Kuril Island and Japan

row channel. It seemed so very close, but most likely was a few miles wide. The overall scenery is overwhelmingly large. It all seems to be out of proportion.

Petropavlovsk Bay was extremely stormy as well and then our big ship's propeller got caught in an underwater net. There was talk that it was a protective device against intruding subs! Now we could go no place and divers had to go in and remove the net. After hours of this activity, the ship had to leave and we never made it to shore. The next morning after breakfast, I was sitting in a whirlpool on the upper deck and looking out of large picture windows over my right side and saw the Kuril Island chain drift by. That is what I call the good life. And then another storm hit us in the Sea of Japan! I love the motions and actions of the sea.

Next stop was Hokkaido, Japan, near Muroran/Sapporo. We ventured into one of Japan's newest volcanic regions, near

Nagasaki, Japan—God, give us Peace!

Mount Usu and went up by cable car towards the crater. Here we saw Japan's newest volcano being born, which began about 60 years ago in a wheat field. That field is now about 300 feet high. Again, the mighty forces of our living planet can be observed if one is willing to do so. We people are not even a blink in the geologic history of our Earth.

"The thing I do most is look at maps. If I am going to a place, I get all the maps and look at them. There is a lot of information on a map!"
PAUL THEROUX

These words of Theroux come right out of my heart, expressing how I feel when preparing a new venture.

Busan, Korea, gave me another look and feel for a different people and culture. The people of this city treated us very well. We were treated to a beautiful dance and musical performance. We then sailed on to Nagasaki, Japan, and the scene of the second infamous atomic disaster caused by mankind. It is incredible what people can do to each other in the defense of an idea or in the defense of power possessed. The Peace Park in that city brings that to light. Our last stop in Asia on this trip was the Osaka Region, where we enjoyed Japanese hospitality, excellent food and good beer. We flew home by plane across the Pacific.

South America—2007-2009: Argentina, Falkland Islands, Tierra del Fuego, Strait of Magellan, Chile, Galapagos

After having traveled in the footsteps of Columbus in the Caribbean region, South America had to follow and again, I am a lucky man to have been able to travel there. Inadvertently, I began to follow in the footsteps of two very famous people, Ferdinand Magellan and Charles Darwin.

In the Wake of the Beagle

The Beagle Channel, Tierra del Fuego

The great city of Buenos Aires gave me a three-day inside view of Argentine life. We toured the city, saw the seat of Government, enjoyed the historical parts and really ate terrific food and drank excellent Malbec wine from the Mendoza Region. A day at a hacienda with Gaucho demonstrations of horse handling and daily life gave us close-up views of their life. In true fashion we were treated to an Argentine Barbeque, with music and dance with young male and female dancers, giving us a chance to participate.

Montevideo in Uruguay gave me a chance, among the local "must do" things, to view the naval monument memorializing the destruction of the German battleship *Graf Spee* in 1939. This was after the first naval battle of The Second World War between Germany and Britain. Then we went on to the Peninsula Valdez. This is one of the largest nature preserves in South America. It is about the size of Massachusetts and is totally dedicated to the preservation of penguins, sea lions, guanacos, rhea and the rare mara (related to the guinea pig, but much larger). There are private sheep farms throughout, but the main emphasis is the preservation of the wildlife. For years there have been migratory whale observations from the cliffs of this peninsula.

Then we steamed through the Atlantic towards the Falkland Islands, where we spent a great time among Gentoo penguins and Tundra geese. The climate in the Falklands is not an easy one to live with, unless of course you were born there. There are constant strong winds, you notice plants and grasses are all bent over, shaking in the strong gusty winds. The sea surface is driven by that same wind and has a strange rippling look to it. And it rains on and off and a bit of sun might also be visible at times. The people treated us with great hospitality and served as guides through the sometimes forlorn countryside. They showed us roped-off areas, where thousands of plastic mines are still burrowed in the soil, leftovers from the Falkland War. They are waiting for technology to handle these plastic mines safely for their removal.

Next goal on this trip was the very famous Cape Horn. A storm already started to form as we left the Falklands and as we approached Terra del Fuego, the storm hit us with a fury, slowing our big ship down to a crawl and delaying our planned arrival at the Cape. We got there at night, with winds at 137 miles per hour. Going out on deck to take pictures of the blinking light of the Horn's lighthouse proved to be an adventure and almost blew us off the deck. The fury of the joining of the forces of the Pacific Ocean, the Atlantic Ocean and the Southern Ocean gives knowledge to the fact that this is one of the most feared sea regions in the world. There is the story of Captain Bligh's second voyage, when he was ordered to get breadfruit saplings from the South Pacific and take them to the Caribbean as future food for the black slaves there. Captain Bligh tried to round the Horn 13 times and failed. His crew was exhausted, the Sea had beat them time and time again. So he announced to the cheering crew, "We will turn around!" . . . but to their great disappointment he decided to reach the South Pacific going around Africa instead!

We left the Cape and went into a channel and the next morning we were baptized with seawater by Neptune (the ship's captain) to honor those of us that had never been there. We spent

Top: The Fury of the Southern Ocean

Glacier in Chile, at Campo Del Hielo Sur

a day in Ushuaia, the world's southernmost town—the starting and supply point of most Antarctic Expeditions and Cruises. In Punta Arenas, Chile, I paid my respects to Magellan by putting my hands on the statue that stands there, erected in his honor.

The Beagle Channel gave us a pleasant day with one of the most fantastic mountain sceneries anywhere in the world, all held together by the sea, reflected from the sky above. The sea animals in masses, islands just covered with bodies of sea lions and Antarctic fur seals. Sailing through the Strait of Magellan from East to West made my mind wander, thinking how Magellan sailed these waters for the first time by western people, wondering after every bend in the channels what might be laying ahead of him. Will he be really coming out on the Pacific side of South America? I was thinking of the young naturalist Charles Darwin, who by the grace of Captain Fitz Roy was on board the *Beagle*, exclaiming about the natural wonders of this region of the world. I could hear my one cartographer friend saying to me, "How many times have I put the name *Strait of Magellan* by hand onto a map and you were physically there!" As I have said, I am a fortunate and lucky man. After we entered the Pacific Ocean, we then sailed North within the inner passages of Chile. We sailed for over 500 miles past one of the world's largest ice fields outside of the Himalayas, this one called *Campo Del Hielo Sur.* There were glaciers and glaciers and more glaciers in all sizes—wide, tall, narrow, steep, majestic, colorful, overwhelmingly beautiful and breathtaking. It made Alaska look small.

We stopped in Puerto Chacabuco, Chile, took a pre-arranged local ride up into the Andes and kayaked among the mighty peaks of the Andes following some streams and lakes and watching the morning fog lift and fall all around us within the silence of nature. After some more stops along the Chilean coast, again enjoying the hospitality of the people of Chile, we disembarked in Valparaiso and went on to Santiago de Chile. From there we ventured up into the Andes toward Mount Aconcagua, which at 22,841 feet is the highest mountain in the Americas. We followed the Aconcagua River and after many switchbacks on a road without guardrails, we reached a little jewel of a lake, Lago Inca at Portillo. This was at about 10,000 feet elevation and we had a great view of the mountain massif. We ate lunch and did not move too much in the thin air. After sightseeing for two more days we left for home. In my heart are very deep impressions about this South American region called Patagonia.

"Travel is the best way we have of rescuing the humanity of places and saving them from abstraction and ideology."
PICO IYER

Ecuador and the Galapagos Islands

As my good fortune would have it, the chance to get to the enchanted Galapagos Islands presented itself and on we went. It was February-March 2009. Flying into Quito is no easy task for any good pilot. The current International Airport is situated on the central plateau of the city, in a North/South configuration, flanked on each side by mountain ranges. The pilot had to rely totally on his instruments, in driving rain, in the middle of the night. Fortunately for us he did a fine job.

At over 9,000 feet elevation, Quito is one of the highest capitals in the world. The thin air was noticed immediately,

Volcano Cotacachi, NE Ecuador

fast movement on our part required extra breathing. Now we were back into the Andes Mountains, this time in the northern part of the continent. We traversed for three days through the northeastern part of Ecuador, touching on one of the Amazon's sources, hiking along dense rainforest along the edge of some small creek. Here we enjoyed the scenery of the Eastern Cordilleras. We overnighted at a thermal spa at 9,000 feet elevation, hiked around a huge crater lake of a once mighty volcano and visited a pre-Inca archeological site, and then physically touched the Equator a few times.

At one point at La Mitad del Mundo, a young guide tried to convince me, *the cartographer and geographer*, that we are presently portraying the Earth in a very false way. The Earth turns around the Equator, therefore our globes and maps should turn, so that North will be to the left and South to the right and of course Ecuador is the center of the world! We visited Otavalo, South America's largest Indian craft market and really enjoyed the very colorful creations of wools, wood, ceramics, jade, fabrics and animal skins. These people do these ancient crafts in a very skillful way and give you their friendly smile as you purchase what they have made.

Ecuador is a beautiful country with great scenery sculpted by the actions of the upwelling of the Andes over the eons. The volcanoes and the erosion have done and are still doing their work shaping the land. As we had arrived in the driving rain days earlier, numerous mudslides had closed most of the roads south and southeast of Quito. The land is very fertile and the agricultural activities of the people are witness to that.

The Galapagos Archipelago

We left Quito to fly to the Galapagos Islands via Quayaquil on AiroGal and arrived in Baltra on the north coast of Santa Cruz. Here the crew of our motor vessel *Pelikano* picked us up. We were 13 passengers and 6 crew members, one of whom was our Ecuadorian Naturalist Juan Carlos. The Ecuadorian Government requires every tourist boat to have a naturalist on board, to assure the safety of the environment and to keep the tourists in line. For eight days we traveled among the major islands of the archipelago being exposed to the wonders of nature that is so unique for island botany and for the Galapagos in particular. The islands are about 600 miles off the shore of South America and were created by tectonic and volcanic forces, never having been part of a continent. Therefore, all major life there has "floated" in over the eons, either by ocean currents or by wind, and developed into their own species. The

Galapagos Marine Iguana

islands are home to birds, sea lions, turtles, tortoises, penguins, iguanas and of course plants.

Some of the islands have very harsh living conditions with no trees or low shrubs. Therefore, very little if any shade is available, baking everything under the equatorial sun. The ground is very difficult to walk on being of volcanic origin and totally uneven with sharp-edged rocks from collapsed small lava tubes. Depending on the cycle of El Nina or El Nino, life either flourishes or dies. Some islands, like Santa Cruz, have great vegetation. The fishing is good and the local fish markets are full of activity. The fishermen offer their catch for sale and the pelicans and iguana walk around them, looking for an opportunity to get some food. Santa Cruz, besides harboring the Darwin Research Station, has its own population of wild tortoises that can be found by walking into the interior of the island.

There are two species of iguana, the land iguana and the marine iguana. They look differently and eat differently. The marine iguana has a much larger population. Before sunrise, we went ashore either by a wet landing or landing on some small natural stone pier, almost always being greeted by a committee of sea lions. By mid morning we would go back to our home the *Pelikano* to have lunch and have a siesta. The sun at that time of the day is hot overhead. Then we went snorkeling alongside sea lions, turtles, tropical fish and yes, white-tipped reef sharks. A sunset at sea to me is always very soul touching, being in the Galapagos made it extra special. The setting sun gives different lights to the volcanic silhouettes of the islands, the great frigate birds are sailing close by the boat and a light breeze caresses the face. How lucky a man am I to be able to experience all of this? Then the stars literally explode around you and the Milky Way arches across the overhead sky.

"I find the great thing in this world is not so much where we stand, as in what direction we are moving. To reach the port of heaven, we must sail sometimes with the wind and sometimes against it, but we must sail and not drift nor lie at anchor."

OLIVER WENDELL HOLMES, JR.

In the Meantime, Life Went On and That Was a Good Thing . . .

I was promoted to Director of Cartographic Operations! How about that for an immigrant! I wonder what Duncan would say about this if he was still alive? With that, I started a very vigorous training program at our office, to have the manual drafting methods converted to computer technology.

As long as we can maintain our physical and mental capacities, we will do travel, it surely enriches life.

Chris Heivly, our technical manager, had advised us to use Macintosh computers and Adobe Illustrator for software. I ordered two computers per month and then took two people off production to have them trained. Sid had all sorts of difficulty understanding and then signing off for all that hardware, software and consequent servers and other support personnel! This allowed us to have our professional cartographers computer trained rather than simply someone who was a computer "geek." We very quickly established our house as a recognized leader in that cartographic technology.

In 1990 I was chosen, together with Scott Edmonds from Maryland Cartographic, a small competitor, to represent American Cartography at a Japanese/American Social Studies Conference in Japan. We were a group of 16 people representing large educational publishers in the United States and us, the two cartographers. We went to Tokyo for a three-day conference. The aim was to disseminate information in regard to Social Studies education in the two countries. Mapmaking has always been a very integral part of our geography and history books in the United States.

Scott Edmonds and I were to give our presentation one after the other. The evening before, I was called to Scott's room. Here I found out that he was ill. He had a problem with the Japanese food, especially the raw fish. He was not in very good shape and asked me if I could do his presentation for him at the conference. I just asked him what his company was worth in money if I wanted to buy it. He replied, "You can have it," he was that ill. Well, as life turned out, that reply would meet him again some time later!

I did Scott's presentation and then my own; both were very well received. Our delegation was given top-level VIP treatment by the government. They gave us a very close look at modern Japanese society. Top entertainment was given to us, including all sorts of strange dishes of various sushi and sashimi. After the conference, we went by bullet train to Kyoto to visit the old imperial capital. Our hosts arranged overnight stays for all of us at various private homes. I stayed in the home of a college professor, with his wife and teenage daughter. As guest of honor, I was served all the food first and afterwards, they prepared the traditional Japanese hot tub for me—a deep bathtub, filled with very hot water. A wooden board across the sides of the tub serves as an armrest, the water goes to your throat. Before you enter the tub, you shower and soap your body so that the bath water stays clean. After the guest of honor took his bath, the rest of the family took theirs. They don't waste water. The woman of the house had prepared my on-the-floor bedding. It was a very comfortable bed and I slept like a baby. The next day, we flew to Hiroshima in order to see the atomic bomb museum. We stayed overnight at a very fine hotel and then went back to Tokyo by plane. Another day visit there and then back home on a non-stop, 16-hour flight to Newark. This was a very interesting learning experience for all of us.

During the late 1980s I started to attend the Frankfurt Book Fair on an annual basis. I started to establish new personal and professional contacts with map publishers in Europe. Once, every other year, Heidi would come along and spend some time with her small family in Frankfurt. Heidi would also assist us at the book fair by manning our sales booth, this way

Look how deep that no-man's-land was on the communist side!

This was the West side of the wall with graffiti.

Heidi and Herwig on the West side of the Berlin Wall, 1988.

giving some of us a chance to either attend a meeting or take a break. In 1988, Heidi and I decided to visit Berlin. I wanted to show Heidi all the spots of my escape in 1955. We stayed in a very nice hotel in Charlottenburg. I took Heidi to the street where Wolfgang and I did our famous "run" into West Berlin. Of course now there was the Berlin Wall!

Nearby was an observation platform. From that vantage point we could look over The Wall. There were actually two walls, the outer wall facing West Berlin separated by the inner wall facing East Berlin. In the middle was the infamous "Death Strip," containing the minefield. Every few hundred yards stood a watchtower, with one-way mirror glass on the top, from which the border guards did their observations with field glasses. Inside the "Western Wall" was a walkway with two guards who would patrol together with guard dogs. Whenever I trained my video camera on them, they would try to hide out of the camera angle. I got them anyway. All the time the tower guard was looking at us, we could see his shadowy outline. In the far distance was the bridge over which Wolfgang and I had crossed. I have the video and also photographs of this trip. As I stood there with Heidi, all kinds of thoughts went through my mind. Thoughts going back to our escape and of course also thoughts about the awful contraption we were looking at. They killed people here!

A government shutting in their people from the rest of the world, under the mantel of "protection," is never good. Whenever any government tries to "protect" its people from bad influences, one should immediately become cautious. This is the first sign of a developing dictatorship! This is

Looking into the "Death Strip," the Schilling Brücke *is middle-center. See guard at the bottom of the wall to the right! (1988)*

usually an attack on human rights and personal freedom. A government should protect the nation as a whole from a direct outside attack, but NEVER individual citizens or citizen groups. Never! Think with me: 173 Germans were killed along the Berlin Wall by Germans and over 600 Germans were killed by Germans along the borders between the two German States! That is horrible! . . . *Time to pause* . . . I thought the Wall would be there much longer. How wrong was I and how great this all ended. The world of international communism was coming apart at its seams. This had been one of the most brutal dictatorships the world had ever lived through and also one of the largest. As we know from human history, the human spirit is strong and usually will outlive any suppression. Sooner or later the oppressor will be overthrown.

The famous words of our President Ronald Reagan to Mr. Gorbachev of the Soviet Union, spoken at the Wall in Berlin, still ring today: *"Mr. Gorbachev, tear down this wall!"* The people in the Eastern countries surrounding East Germany started to get rid of their rulers. The Wall in Berlin came down and the people in that part of Germany all of a sudden experienced something they had not enjoyed since the end of The Second World War—True Freedom! I saw a picture of President Reagan hammering at the Berlin Wall and so I had to follow him and do the same!

Heidi and I visited my nephew Peter Reichel in Leipzig. His wife Martina, Heidi and I went by train to Berlin and we had a hammer and a chisel with us. The train trip took us through some of the towns were I had lived as a young man during my years of school and cartographic training; Weimar, Gotha and Erfurt. When the train stopped, I threw an American penny on the tracks, to reconnect me with my past. I also observed the leftover border guards of this fast fading communist regime and it raised my blood pressure just looking at these people.

As a citizen of the United States, we were forced to cross into East Berlin using the famous Checkpoint Charley. We had tried to go through the Brandenburg Gate, but we were stopped. It was the last time that a border guard on the east side would harass me—"Do not use your video camera here!" We collected a piece of bulletproof glass from one of the long walkways through which they used to channel visitors. As soon as I was at the Wall, I attacked it with vigor and a lot of inner joy, frustration and yes, some anger!

Herwig hammering the Berlin Wall in 1990.

The West German Government under Chancellor Kohl did the only right thing by going head first into the reunion process. Germany's future was at stake here and he had vision enough to see this and press on with it, no matter what the cost. Of course, a number of people did not agree with that policy, for whatever reason, and that is ok; one cannot please all the people.

The whole German economy received a setback, because of the heavy financial burden and resulting drain on the budget. This is the material side of the reunion; the emotional side is a totally different matter. It will take a whole generation or more, before the German people will again be feeling as one nation.

Our own politicians here did not give this whole process of the downfall of communism the attention and loud support that it so urgently deserved. President George H. W. Bush (#41), in my humble opinion, was way cautious in his reaction to these profound changes taking place at the time. This was a very important time in the general history of mankind. Millions of people had died and hundreds of millions were enslaved for decades, but they were freed by the process of American Democracy, as advocated by Ronald Reagan.

Perhaps Bush was under the influence of the American media. These people had treated the communists with soft gloves. They had lectured the American public to respect and fear the "mighty Soviet Union" and had consistently treated the Soviets as equals to us Americans. They had fallen for their propaganda and never understood the shallow nature of the communist system. For reasons that I never understood, they never caught on to the brutal terror that was ruling nations for so many decades. Only Nazi Germany was always THE villain, never Stalin and never Mao. People who lived within that system knew better. Go back and read what I was talking about in the opening chapters about the removal of 11 million people. That was only Germany, there were many more.

My brother-in-law Harry picked us up in Leipzig and he took us to his home, so that I could visit with my sister Traute. The landscape was an eye opener! We traveled through the East German bituminous coal region, where during the communist era the coal was being mined in the open-pit method, to satisfy the energy use of the country. They had literally raped the Earth! For miles there was nothing but gray dirt, like the surface of the moon. Huge scraping machines were standing there. The air was loaded with dust particles, so much so that Harry had to turn on the headlights of the car in the daytime. The Pleisse River (a large river in Saxony) was a dead body of water, devoid of any life. We rode through the town of Zwickau and I noticed the bullet holes from the fighting of World War II still in all the buildings. There was nothing but total neglect and destruction of the environment, the pay-off of over 40 years of communist rule.

Today communist China is doing the same thing and again, nobody seems to care. As a matter of fact, we here in the U.S.A. are being told that *we* are ruining the Earth! People should travel more, with open eyes and open ears and see what is going on in other parts of the world.

As I said before, Heidi and I had started to take up more travel for pleasure and we did a number of wonderfully relaxing trips into the eastern Caribbean region. After 1989 we did a 1992, 1993, 1995 and 1998 sailing trip, which were followed by three trips to swim with humpback whales off the Dominican Republic and two times swimming with Atlantic Spotted Dolphins in the Bahamas, all the time on the beautiful ocean catamaran *Bottom Time II* from Ft. Lauderdale, Florida.

Heidi the Human Dolphin in Bimini.

In May 1993 came another remarkable event in my life. My two dear cousins Gertrud and Helga asked me if I would join them in a trip to Memelland. Boy did I jump at that opportunity! This would be my chance to go back to Laudschen. Of course I said yes and I persuaded Heidi to come along. I had told her so many things about my childhood and now she would be able to relate better to all that. I also asked my brother and my sister to come along, but they declined. Wolfgang was getting weaker from all his illnesses and Traute had no wish to go back to the past.

My brother was physically never a very strong man. As a child, he had fallen into freezing water when he was ice skating and contracted a very bad lung infection. They had to open his chest from the back, by removing one part of a rib, in order to insert a hose to start the drainage of fluid.

Well, while he was still a teenager, he started to smoke

cigarettes and did that for the rest of his life. Later in life, he started to drink a lot of alcohol. All that combined destroyed his health and he died in December 1993. Way too young. Like all of us, he had dreams—like sailing around the world. His ashes were buried in a sea burial off the town of Travemünde/Schleswig Holstein, Germany. He loved the Baltic Sea and often had fished in that area.

A Trip Home to My Birthplace—1993

My two cousins had many friends in Lithuania and together they made all sorts of arrangements. We arrived in Vilnius, the capital, via plane and a whole group of young and older people were there to greet us excitedly. The next two weeks turned out to be very memorable ones in my life.

We were taken to one of their friends' apartments and had a feast with food, caviar and champagne. We knew what that meant to these people. This is a very poor country and we were sure they all spent a lot of money on us, which they really could not afford. For the night's sleep we were put up in various apartments, for housing was extremely tight. After another day of sightseeing in Vilnius, they were preparing the city for the upcoming visit by Pope John Paul II.

We went on to Kaunas, the old capital of Lithuania. During our entire stay we never had to use public transportation. There was always somebody to drive us, wherever we had to go. We never slept in a hotel, always with friends. This way, we really got to know the people and their way of life very closely. We were constantly reminded of the terrible occupation by the Russians. These people had suffered so much!

Then we left Kaunas and were driven along the banks of the Memel River (now Njemen) toward our old county seat of Heydekrug (now Silute). There were all kinds of feelings in my heart; soon I would be in Laudschen! What would I find there? Would I be able to find my way back to where the schoolhouse was? This would take me back to the time when I was eight years old!

After a day in Heydekrug, we were driven towards Laudschen. The railroad tracks along the main highway were gone, but one could see where they had been. The little train station, from which the four of us had left that dreadful morning in 1944, was also gone. We drove off the highway, took a right at a farmer's house and then we stopped. I was pretty sure that the road I was looking at was leading to the school. We inquired and sure enough that was it. I asked if I could walk from this point to my "home." Our driver left and Heidi and my cousins joined me in that walk back to my childhood!

They had built a new bridge over the River Schusste and I could make out the remnants of the old bridge in the bushes at the riverbanks. We walked past the old willow trees where my father had built the high water footbridge. I was told that his tradition was kept up in bad flooding years out of necessity. Then I saw the house up on the hillside. What a moment in my life. From the distance, I could see the house totally as I remembered it!

The same vines were covering the brick of the south side and the windows were painted white, as we had done. But as we came closer, I started to realize that the house was actually in bad repair. The red roof tiles were broken in many areas and the main structure of the roof showed signs of bad damage, visible by sagging sections. But, the house was there.

A couple of the teachers had gone ahead of us by car and one of them lived in the house. The house was divided into apartments; our old school section was also converted into an apartment. A new school building had been built.

I entered the house from the backside, through the door that looked not any different in appearance and color from my time there. My emotions ran a little crazy, I felt like I was in a trance. I went up the stairs, touching the banister over which I had fallen. We went into the room where we kids had lived and I looked out of the window to the side of the house trying to find a familiar landmark. There were none, all was heavily overgrown with vegetation. I could not see all I wanted to see, because not all the people who lived there now were home. The courtyard also looked familiar in one way and different in others. There were some structures attached to what used to be our old barn.

I walked out of the old schoolyard, away from the house, in order to retrace some old steps and also get another perspective of the building. All kinds of thoughts flooded through my brain. I filled a small container with some soil and stones from the area directly by the house and then bade my silent goodbye.

They drove us to the new schoolhouse. The students had been given some time off, so that they and the teachers could spend time with me and ask us many questions. We laid a foundation that day for future communications. I saw their very poor material for the geography classes and promised to help them. They had one world atlas for the school. The publishing date was 1953 and printed in the Soviet Union. For heaven's sake!

In 1999, the school celebrated their 260th anniversary and they sent me a very nice card and asked me for a picture of my father. In March 2000 I sent them an enlarged picture, together with some map material. Wow, perhaps my father's picture will be hanging in that school, portraying the man who was the last German teacher at that school.

We then drove back to Heydekrug and the next day we started our journey up towards Memel (Klaipeda). The goal was to take the car ferry to Nidden. As we waited for the ferryboat I was wandering around the docks and came to a point that had me startled. I could swear that I stood at or near the spot where in 1944 we had boarded our escape towards Königsberg!

We traveled down the Nehrung up to the Russian border, separating Lithuania from the Russian enclave of Kaliningrad Oblast. The town of Tilsit (yes the cheese was named after that town) is now called Sovietsk. This little remnant of once mighty Prussia is a political and economic nightmare, totally surrounded by nations not very friendly with the Russians. It is hard to imagine what could become of it over the next time period. The Germans and Lithuanians had been driven out by Stalin's conquest and the Russians living there now, are completely isolated from Russia.

We finally made it to Nidden and I found it as I remembered it with small houses and cottage-like buildings, most of them very well kept. Fishing boats at anchor. I saw signs of cultivating the "Kurische Kultur," the tribe of the Kuren were early settlers and fishers of the region. The sand dunes of the

Nehrung bear their name and also the lagoon between Nidden and the mainland. We trekked up the Great Sand Dune of Nidden. Sometimes, when you squint your eyes, you think you are in the Sahara. One of the most intriguing jewelry stones in the world is amber and amber is only found in a very few places in the world. (The Dominican Republic is one of the other places.) The main source for amber has always been the Baltic region and it has always been an important bartering item. The early Greeks called them rays of sunlight. We bought lots of very fine amber jewelry, at very reasonable prices.

We stayed overnight in Memel and the next day went to Polangen (now Palanga) to visit a great amber museum. The collections displayed there are outstanding and very rare in the world. From here we went to Schaulen (now Siauliai) in order to visit the very famous Kreuzberg (Hill of Crosses). This hill had been a very sacred site for the faithful Catholics for many years. People would leave a cross or rosary after they had conducted their prayers. During the Soviet occupation, the people increased their prayers and left symbols of their faith and it had amounted to a very large area of religious displays. The Soviets tried again and again to remove these symbols. What they achieved was to raise the defiance of the population against their oppressors to a much greater scale. This then had become a symbolic expression of freedom for the Lithuanian people. It is a sight to see. There are tens of thousands of crosses and rosaries and other holy figures, etc., on top of each other. During the time of our visit, the people were preparing the site for the upcoming visit by the Pope. We were preceding the Pope by about three weeks and I jokingly said I was checking the places out for him. After going back to Kaunas and Vilnius, we went on home to Germany.

This visit had been a good move for me. It solidified my belief in and understanding of my historical background. It confirmed my knowledge of my roots. It also helped me see that people have to learn to live with each other, even in places some had called their ancestral homes for centuries. East Prussia is no more; there is now Lithuania, Poland and Russia. The Lithuanians are very good caretakers of what they inherited and I liked what I saw. A United Europe should be the answer to all that previous cultural, political and religious strife between nations, people and tribes. There must be hope in the world for people to be able to live in peace and harmony. It does sound utopian, but if we do not have hope for a better life on this planet, what would we have instead?

CHAPTER 12

The End of My Cartographic Life

Here I was, on top of my career, in a top position in my industry, and well recognized in the U.S.A. and abroad. Our Division had a great name both within the company and among our extensive customer list. With great professional performances, we had built up a very fine relationship with the Cartographic Division of the National Geographic Society and their division head, John F. Shupe. Later, as we retired, Jack and I became friends.

Donnelley in the meantime had greatly diversified. No longer was the company just a printer and binder, but had gone into other, related ventures. The financial printing division was growing at a very fast and exciting pace. But there were other things, such as software developing, software industry printing and disc replications at a grand scale. The CEO had grandiose ideas about growth. He said, "By the year 2000 we will be a ten billion dollar company!" Well, rumors started to fly that RRD will start selling off certain groups or divisions. Guess who was used as a trial balloon? The Cartographic Division was sold to a California financial interest group and was to be known as GeoSystems. Everybody above a certain age was told to retire and that included yours truly. I was 58 years old!

It was just plain incredible how they handled this situation for all of us "old" people. No severance package of any kind was offered. Your years of service and your last salary would determine the pension you were going to get! Take it or quit. If they would have kept me on for three more years, my pension would have been substantial enough to have kept me afloat with another small job. I received 20% of the pension once promised. I am sorry to say it, but companies know that and cut people like me much earlier in order to save money. It's a fact. The total bottom line of a corporation looks great at the end! I got major medical insurance for Heidi and I for about $180 per month, not bad but of course no dental plan. This whole thing was just a total shock.

For some reason unknown to me to this day, I was told they would keep me on full salary for six months at GeoSystems. I believe it was the CEO that had made the arrangement. Other than that I heard, "Herwig, we will no longer have a Director for Operations." (This statement was OK for two years; then they again appointed a Director of Operations). They appointed two people, very good friends and colleagues of mine, therefore splitting my job into two positions. I was moved into a small office on the top floor and left to myself. My pride was hurt indeed and I suffered emotionally a lot, but I did not want to show it. Heidi and I were not quite safe financially. I swallowed my pride and made it known that I wanted to help the success of the new company.

September 1, 1994, was my official retirement day. GeoSystems threw a party for me at the Eden Inn here in Lancaster. All sorts of people showed up, including the National Geographic Society. I got from them a large, floor model globe as a present, given to me by Jack Shupe, Chief Cartographer, in person. Who was not at that party? My former employer! Oh well . . .

This is the globe Jack Shupe presented to me from my friends at the National Geographic Cartographic Division.

I Was No Longer a Cartographer

Next, I became an independent consultant. In the spring of 1995 I traveled to England, the Netherlands, Germany, the Czech Republic and Hungary. One year I was in Europe three times. All of this was very good, it kept me in the loop of our profession and I felt that I was needed.

I had recently received a new U.S. passport, as the old one was full and also obsolete. At the *Reise und Verkehrsverlag* in Stuttgart, Germany, I met a man born in Prague. His name was Cerny and he did business arrangements for the publisher. I had some business to do in Prague and he offered to take me there with his car, this way showing off his former home country. When we came to the border crossing between Germany and the Czech Republic, the custom officer asked for my passport. I handed the document to him and when he saw that I was a U.S. citizen, he saluted to me. Then he asked if he could take the passport to his supervisor, since they had not seen the newly issued U.S. passports at that time.

He came back with his superior and they were very animated when talking with me and they wished me a very good time in their country. "Wow," I said to Mr. Cerny, "they must like me." He explained that the people in the Czech Republic revere Americans and their culture. When we drove through the country, most music over the car radio was Western and Blue Grass! It was the month of May and the whole land was painted in the various greens of spring, interspersed with large fields of very yellow rape plants. They grow that for the healthy oil. As we turned a corner of the country road at one point, we came upon some people in very colorful customs and there was also a large May Tree (a spring custom in parts of Germany and Eastern Europe) in the center of the village square. We really slowed down and then were stopped by a very nice young lady holding a decorated tray with some wine glasses. She said, "Please accept the drink and join us in the party." They were celebrating a wedding. We parked the car, had some wine and before long, we were dancing with the people to the tunes played by a small band.

Then we continued on to Prague. This is one of the very few European cities not damaged by The Second World War. Downtown is a picture book of medieval architecture at its finest. The old, large castle of the Bohemian Kings watches on a very high rise over the city. It also houses the residence of the current President of the Republic. The uniform of the guard at the entrance gate looked sort of familiar to me and I mentioned that to Cerny. He told me to look closely. It was a total replica of a U.S. Marine dress uniform. I spent three days in Prague, and in Mr. Cerny I had a fine guide and host! This was a great place to visit and spend time.

The company decided to go into publishing. For that they needed to produce their own products. I was asked if I would be willing to help establish the procedures and networks necessary to do so in exchange for a full-time position. I accepted and became the Manufacturing Manager of this new venture. I was a one-man band! I was back in full working life. The company bought another well-known geographic product distribution firm in Cambridge, MA. By combining this firm with the manufacturing arm, we became the Publication Group, now about 15 people strong.

My sons in the meantime did go forward with their own lives, becoming successful in their own ventures and professions. I am very proud of their accomplishments—Michael in the business world and Peter in education. They married and produced two children each—beautiful and great Megan and Erik in Seattle and beautiful and great Maggie and Hannah in Macungie—therefore enlarging my direct family here in the U.S.A.

I immersed myself deeply into the printing business and I had to travel quite a bit at times. I spent time in Spain and Germany to print for either National Geographic or some other customers in Europe of GeoSystems. I spent weeks in Quebec, Canada, at Transcontinental Printing, again primarily printing for NGS. I was in Ohio, Massachusetts, Florida and Pennsylvania and I became known as an expert in "press O.K.'s" and as a "color coordinator."

Herwig O.K.'s NGS Road Atlas at Detroit press in 1997.

The body of a book or an atlas is produced in sections; printers call it "signatures." Depending on the size and volume of a book and also the way it was bound, signatures can be 4, 8, 16 or 32 pages. Color O.K.'s are needed to assure the desired strength of the colors and the general balance throughout a book. Whenever the head pressman thinks that the color is O.K., he calls for the customer, in this case me, representing our publisher. I would then look over the pages looking for the above-mentioned criteria. After having given the O.K., the press starts to roll until that "sig" is finished. Then I waited until the next "sig" was being readied and I would be asked again. These periods of waiting can be either short or long, depending on the total run of the book. 10,000 books take a certain period of time, while 100,000 books takes a lot longer. Sometimes my waiting time would be 3-4 hours, which was the time to catch up on some sleep.

Printing presses normally run 24/7 or 24/6. Sometimes I spent days at the plant, never to see my hotel room. I have slept or dosed off on plastic couches, soft chairs, hard chairs—you name it. For a pillow, I sometimes would roll a bundle of printed paper and put it under my neck. Oftentimes, there was no chance whatsoever to sleep. One O.K. after another for 32 hours—that was my record!

The printing companies usually treated people like me very well. After all, a satisfied customer might bring back more business. I have been in very fine hotels and have eaten in very fine restaurants everywhere. But it could also go this way: One time I checked into a hotel. They had given me the "top flight" suite. When I dropped my bag in and saw it I thought whoa, this will be great! Then I went to the plant. Two days later I went back to the hotel to pick up my bag—I never slept or ate there!

I was also asked to assist the company, together with some other representatives, at the Frankfurt, Germany, Annual Book Fair and I did this six years in a row. Being fluent in the German language, knowing Frankfurt well and having had contacts with various European companies was considered a great help. Usually one colleague and I would be first in Frankfurt to set up the display booth; the other members of our crew would arrive a day later. The Frankfurt Book Fair was a very hard thing to do. The different halls of the Fair are spread out over acres of space and we would split up the various appointments with current or prospective customers. That alone resulted very often into bodily sprints from one hall to another, carrying sample books and a computer, dressed in a suit and perspiring like crazy! One morning I had an appointment with a Russian publisher. After we exchanged greetings and had sat down, one of the gentlemen produced a bottle of vodka and a set of glasses. They poured the drinks. I told them that it is 9:30 in the morning and is too early to drink alcohol. They said, "It is never too early to drink vodka! Cheers and let's have a fine meeting, after another vodka."

Then, at the end of the day, we had to shut down all the electronics and lights, pack our computers and usually walk toward the main Frankfurt train station, about eight city blocks away, because the cabs and the public transports were totally overrun by the public and the thousands of visitors and customers at the Fair. We then had to find a place where we could get a meal, not easy during Fair time in Frankfurt. And all of that for five days! Being away from Heidi became more and more difficult. The older we get, the closer we are getting to each other. Also as I got older, I noticed that I had trouble driving at night, especially in rain.

In 1999, GeoSystems was renamed MapQuest.com and in May of that year the company was taken public. Some management people had joined the company from the outside and the whole structure, expectantly, started to change. Those people and a few from our company with their given stock holdings, were now potential millionaires. A major on-line company in turn bought the whole company. That was the end of that chapter!

And here is what that on-line company did to MapQuest:

They took the MapQuest arm (the e-routing) out of the cartographic arm and established that as an independent unit. Then they cancelled the contract with National Geographic as it was deemed too costly for the company. In 2001, they closed down the entire Publishing Group. All of us in that unit were out of a job at once. I said to myself, *This is it. I will not work for anybody anymore I am retiring for good. No more you must go there. No more you must represent. No more pleasing a boss. No more watching the bottom line of business. I will have personal freedom of life.*

The next thing that happened to me was that I had cataracts removed from my eyes and replaced with artificial lenses! My eyesight at the moment is the best it has ever been in my entire life. Now I could snorkel with a regular mask and see the wonders of the sea below! We went with our dear friends Rick

Humpback Close to Our Zodiak

and Sandy Kellam on another humpback whale trip in 2004. Swimming with a regular snorkel mask was wonderful and I could see everything!

Heidi and I decided to start enjoying life more than we already had learned to do. Heidi was still very involved in her swimming and singing programs at various pools for one and various churches and singing organizations for the other. That was good. One has to stay among people and do things for the soul. Besides, Heidi's involvement in these groups was appreciated. I always enjoyed Heidi's music, through her I had learned to know a lot about composers and their works. I also learned about the conductors that made that possible. Throughout the years we made many friends this way. Heidi is now singing for churches in a choir or as a soloist, or she participates in choral work for either churches or choral groups. In 2000 she joined the chorus of the Lancaster Symphony and in addition became a member of the chorus at the Ephrata Cloister. I myself started to enjoy swimming more

Penguins, Falkland Islands

Antarctic Fur Seals, Beagle Channel

and more and I remember very well when I swam my first full mile, which was in the spring of 2003!

Photography, connected with the use of the computer, is something I enjoy doing. I love to be outside and enjoy nature in all its glory. I love to watch ice hockey on the TV and have been doing that for 35 years.

Heidi loves to sew, knit and crotchet and both of us love to cook. The rule is: One cooks and the other one cleans up. We also love to read. We read almost anything, but we love history or a good novel, biographies and great travel stories.

Thanks to the world of the internet I am in close contact with my niece Angela Laufer in Frankfurt. She and I sometimes speak for over an hour and a half on the phone; she needs a father figure. My nephew Roland Schutzler, who is also in Frankfurt, tries to stay in contact with us in his own way although he is a very lazy writer, on the computer or in postal mail. Unfortunately he developed MS, the so-called slow version, and tries to deal with this as best as he can. His faithful life's companion, Ute Henn, tries to keep the contact with us open. Of course there is my dear cousin Gertrud Schimanke in Darmstadt, and there was Helga, her sister in Ludwigshafen who died of breast cancer in 2005.

My sister Traute will be 79 years of age this August. She lost her husband Harry last year to all sorts of Diabetes-related illnesses. She herself moves rather slowly; she is a bit heavy. Her son Peter Reichel, who lives in Leipzig, visits with her every two weeks and gets groceries for her, etc. He had been operated on for throat cancer last year and is battling that recovery. But he still smokes cigarettes!

Helga being as sick as she was, asked us to come and visit them at Christmas in 2004. We did and this was the first time for us to be in Germany at Christmas since 1960! That was great. Helga was so happy to see us and we spent some great time with her. We had some wonderful days together. Christmas Eve we went to church with Gertrud's grandchildren. We also visited the Christkindel Market in Frankfurt and in Darmstadt and drank *Glühwein* (hot wine, with the aroma of cloves and cinnamon). New Year's Eve was literally a blast. German citizens shoot off a lot of fireworks all over town, in all directions. Taking videos of that event was not without hazards.

I am now in my 70s and except for some painful arthritis, I am in good health. Heidi battles the strange joint virus she had developed four years ago and some of that seems to "settle" into arthritis, and some serious problems with her right foot. She had injured the ankle in a bad misstep and nasty twist stepping into a hole at Peter's house and it created so many problems she had to give up teaching water aerobics! Then they discovered, way too late, that she had broken the top middle joint of the foot, either then or at some other point. That explained all the continuous pain she had. We hope that there will be some relief at one time or another. Then they discovered spinal stenosis, the source of a lot of pain, and a deteriorated hip joint. Now, what should be fixed first?

We enjoy life, we enjoy the company of each other, we like our house and friends and we appreciate that at least one son lives close to us and we can visit the grandchildren and follow how they grow up. Love is a wonderful event in a person's life, but there is also the other love, the love and understanding that people should let freely flow and not mask under the strain of the hectic modern life.

I have become an active member of our church, the UCC Church of the Apostles, as a council member and commission member and I hope that I can apply my life experiences with its successes and failures in a positive way. My life has been full of events of personal nature and through the course of history has often touched on international events. I have never regretted having moved from Europe to North America. I do belong here and I feel at home here.

The 2000s years are rolling along quite well. Heidi and I travel now even more, the philosophy being: Do it while you still can. In 1995, we went with Gertrud and Helga on an extensive trip back to my homeland. I have written a comprehensive log on that event. We went one more time back to the humpback whales in 2004. Although that time Heidi's neck was seriously injured riding the fast zodiacs bouncing in the waves. We had great experiences, but Heidi paid a price. In the fall of 2005 we went on our first cruise, called the Transpacific Odyssey, which took three weeks. Taking us from Seattle, to Alaska, across the Bering Sea to the Kamchatka Peninsula, on to Korea and Japan and then back to Seattle. When we came back, Helga had died of breast cancer. She had valiantly battled that illness for about four years. Now we really appreciated that we went to Germany at Christmas in 2004, seeing her for the last time.

I keep a very close phone contact with Gertrud now. She needed someone to talk to after giving Helga personal hospice care in her home for nine months. All her siblings have died except one brother, Alfred, who had removed himself from the entire family many years ago and she has no contact with him. Whatever comes next, will come. Heidi and I have had the fortune to be able to live a long life, full of dramatic events and I was able to write about it.

March 2008—A Few *Recent* Important Events Have to Be Inserted Here

In March/April 2007, Heidi and I were on an extended trip to Patagonia. We were in Buenos Aires when we got a phone call from Gertrud to the effect that my sister Traute had died. I contacted our son Peter and asked him to be my go-between until we came back from our trip. He did a very fine job doing what had and could be done. As soon as we came back, I phoned my nephew Peter Reichel and he and I decided that I would not travel to Germany. Instead I would do that another day, when all is calm again.

Then came another blow. My nephew Roland Schutzler was diagnosed with MS. Now a trip to Germany took on more of an urgency. Traute is no longer around, Peter R. is still battling his throat cancer and Roland is now also vulner-

At Brandenburg Gate

Peter & Herwig on the Schilling-brücke Bridge

able. I decided to go as soon as I could do it. Upon mentioning this to our son Peter, he asked if he could come along. As a matter of fact, he asked me if we could fly with a stop in Berlin, so that he would have a chance to go with me to the spot where my brother and I had crossed the border so many years earlier.

So, he and I went on this (for me very emotional) trip. I took Peter to the most important sites of Berlin, including the bridge Wolfgang and I crossed in 1955. We had dinner one evening with a former business friend of mine. Peter's German language skills came back real fast! He really impressed me and the rest of the family! In our travels in and through the former East German Republic (what an aberration that was), I tried hard to get Peter to understand where and how we had lived back then.

Left: Katarina Reichel

Right: Herwig, Peter R. & Peter S. at the Völkerschlacht *Monument.*

Larissa, Anneliese & Susi

Peter S., Peter Laufer, Roland & Ute Henn

Tim, Peter & Angela Laufer

Peter S.
& Roland

Peter S.
& Gertrud

Sipping a PILS under a fresh garland of hops!

From Berlin we traveled by train to Leipzig and spent a couple of days with my nephew Peter Reichel, his daughter Katarina, and his girlfriend Christa. We toured Leipzig one day with Peter R., and one day on a city tour bus as tourists, and of course we talked a lot about family. Peter R. had complained to me that his mother had withheld from him information of family members, especially his grandfather Heinrich Schutzler, my father. We went to visit the famous *Völkerschlacht Denkmal* at the edge of the city. My son Peter was in awe when he saw this grand building, that was erected as a monument to the Battle of Leipzig in 1813 between Napoleon's Army and the combined Armies of Prussia, Austria and Russia. It is quite a magnificent structure.

Then we took another train trip across Germany to Frankfurt/Main in order to meet with Roland and Angela. The trip from Leipzig gave my son Peter a chance to see what used to be East Germany. We traveled through Erfurt and Gotha and Eisenach (Wartburg). This way my life story became very vivid to him.

The day we arrived in Frankfurt, my brother-in-law Jose Huici-Astiz died unexpectedly of a pulmonary embolism. Things were really hitting me left and right! We met with Anneliese (Heidi's sister), Susi and Larissa (her daughter and granddaughter) in a café in downtown Frankfurt. In the meantime, we stayed at Angela (my niece) and Peter Laufer's house and again had long talking sessions with Roland and Angela and others. That was good for us all, especially our son Peter, who had not been back to Germany since he had graduated from high school.

Then we went on to Darmstadt to visit with Gertrud. After one more day Peter flew home and I followed two days later. It was a whirlwind of a trip that left various impressions on many family members. People were so happy to have seen Peter and wanted to stay in touch with him. Peter himself was so taken in by what he had seen he told me, "I will take my family to Germany very soon, perhaps next year."

A Very Serious Health Problem Affecting Heidi Put Another Hurdle Into Both Our Lives

In the winter of 2008-09, it was discovered that Heidi needed surgery on her lower spine and it was suggested that the four lower vertebrae should be fused, since some serious stenosis was deforming the bones. The nerve flow was impeded and she would face life in a wheelchair!

Therefore, we decided to go on one big trip, not knowing what Heidi's physical abilities would be like in the future. Besides, 2009 was the 50th Anniversary of our marriage. No other plans had been made for this occasion. Our family physician is an avid traveler and often takes people along on his trips. We joined his travel group to Ecuador and then on to the Galapagos Islands at the end of February 2009. Some extra cortisone seemed to give Heidi some pain relief, on top of the extra flow of adrenaline.

Four and half months after our return, Heidi's lower spine was fused during five and half hours of surgery. Six long screws (they look like deck screws) and three pieces of titanium were holding the "new" spine together. Against our advice and repeated reminders of Heidi's allergies, the wound was closed with nylon stitches, resulting in a bad infection that kept part of the incision open for seven weeks. When she started to exercise and move about, she noticed she still had a lot of pain in the back and hip area. More consultations and x-rays were taken. Heidi has a good friend who is a veterinary technician. Heidi was showing her the x-ray of the "screwed back" and her friend says, "Has anybody told you, you have a very bad hip joint?" By this time, Heidi was walking with a cane. We went to see another surgeon and he, looking at the new x-rays says, "How are you able to walk on a cracked hip joint?" Six months later a total hip replacement was done very successfully! All of that started with a misdiagnosed broken bone in her right foot!

With a lot of willpower and good water exercises, Heidi is back swimming and singing again! But not without some restrictions, like not standing too long on her feet or sitting down too long and certain strokes while swimming. We think being on sailing boats will not be advisable for Heidi ever again. Well, I certainly was wrong about that at the time! But, overall, life is still good for us. We have each other, we are not victims of some nasty disease and we can participate in life fully and help others.

Having lived in Lancaster for over forty years now makes this our home base. We have many caring friends, and we know the merchants, the banks and the doctors. We are active in the community, Heidi through her singing with the local symphony and some other groups and teaching aqua fitness and I being active in my church, elected to the council and a commission. We go to the theater, enjoy symphony concerts, or go on day trips or week trips to visit friends in Maine or Florida.

Heidi Schutzler as the "Mechanical Doll" in the Tales of Hoffmann, *by Offenbach, 1978.*

Carmina Burana *in 2011 was such an event.*

The performance required over 200 musicians and three soloists.

At age 73, Heidi is still singing with the Symphony chorus every year, very remarkable indeed, considering all the physical problems she had. I always said her voice is a God-given gift and that might explain how she can still do all this at this time in her life. Heidi has given so much to people all over our entire living area, in solo concerts, choral concerts and her aria performances in the operas.

We have traveled extensively, we both have been engaged in all sorts of activities throughout our lives and in so doing, we have met a lot of people that resulted in establishing very solid friendships with like-minded people, giving us the pleasure of hearing other ideas or solidifying our own observations. There are so many individuals here in PA, in Maryland, in Florida and in New Jersey we call close friends. These friendships we do cherish quite a lot, especially since we have a rather small family here in the States. So, Heidi and I look at our friends as our extended family.

An Amish Farmer Near Strasburg, PA

One Other Important Phase of Our Life Has to Be Mentioned Here

Heidi had been working as a bilingual tour guide for a local tourist attraction called "The Amish Farm & House." She saw the need for a printed German language guide for the many German tourists that arrived here every summer. That published book had her name and phone number on the inside cover. One day a man with a strong voice called; I answered. He wanted to speak with Heidi. He explained to her that he was working on a book that he wanted to publish describing the origin of the well-known Amish hymnal called *Der Ausbund*. He wanted to meet with her and he introduced himself as Ben Blank of Narvon, PA.

We met him at the Mennonite Historical Library here in town, where he described his need for help in his dealings with the German Catholic Church and Museum in Passau, Germany. Ben Blank turned out to be a very special human being. He was a retired farmer and an active preacher in his Amish Community. He was a very well-read man having tremendous knowledge of history, world events and the human psyche. Besides that he was a great Christian man, who dearly loved his wife Annie. He invited us to visit with his wife. Out of that visit grew a very close friendship between Heidi and Annie that lasted until God called Annie and Ben home.

Heidi helped Ben by making phone calls and writing letters to various people in Passau, Germany. In the cellars of the famous castle of Passau the early Anabaptists had been incarcerated in the very early 1700s for five years and there they wrote the words to the *Ausbund*! Ben's book was published in 2001 under the title of *The Amazing Story of the Ausbund.* Not bad for a man with an eighth-grade education! He wrote two more books, *Creation to Resurrection* and *The Scriptures Have the Answers.* He also initiated the translation of a 160-year-old Amish religious manual written in German, which took Heidi and me two years to complete. The title of the book is *Das Wahre Christenthum, True Christianity.* Annie and her daughters rewarded our labor of love with a wonderful, hand-made quilt.

Over the years we have come to know Ben and Annie's children and their families and also have become close friends with their daughter Fannie, her husband Steve and their fine children. We see each other quite regularly. Let me elaborate on this a bit further. I am looking at the friendship we have with Steve and Fannie as a gift from God. Through Ben and Annie Blank we got to know these fine people—we are now sort of an adopted arm of their families. This helps tremendously in our loneliness as immigrants, with very little family of our own.

Ben's younger son Steve and his brothers and all the families always open their arms to Heidi and I, as if we were family. They in turn had the book *Das Wahre Christenthum* printed and published in 2009 and gave Heidi a special copy signed by all of Ben and Annie's children.

I developed inflammatory arthritis first in both hands and then also in my right and left shoulder in early 2009. It became very painful and I was put on a mild dose of steroids. I needed to function properly, because Heidi needed all the help I could give her, to help her through two major surgeries and all the after activities. At the end of November 2010, I got off the steroids and the next two months developed into painful hell for me. I lost all strength in both hands and the whole right arm. Heidi had to help dress and undress me and I could no longer do work around the house.

After another meeting with our physician, I got back on another round of steroids (.75mg per pill, 10 days three per day, thereafter 2 per day). It was February 2011 and I had to wait and see how this would proceed. At the moment I was a functioning human being again, thanks to cortisone. *(I had no idea what fate had in store for me not much later!)*

I am thankful for the existence of the United States of America. This country has given me a chance to make a good living, to establish and maintain a family and to be able to raise two new valuable members for our society. I have lived under three different political systems and I have traveled over a good part of our globe seeing and comparing other countries, systems and customs. Our democratic system, founded over 200 years ago based on strong moral principals, is currently the best in the world. It is still the hope and beacon to millions of people throughout the world, as it was to my brother and me, back in 1955. That is why so many are still trying to sneak in every day! I am astonished to hear some politicians in Washington, D.C., tearing down our country and its achievements in their speeches. Thousands upon thousands of American soldiers lost their lives in the

God Bless America!

defense of Europe and many more were crippled for life. The United States can be very proud of its accomplishments in war and in peace. Every country has enemies, war or no war. But to the world, we should be Americans and these political power-happy people no longer care about that. It hurts all of us in the long run, including these people.

The Following Is Material Written in Later Years—Thoughts About Life in the 21st Century

(Written in the fall of 2011)

I am 75 years of age and I believe my mental capacities are not diminished in any way. So, I believe I can still say things that count, in my opinion. I am watching with astonishment how our society has been developing in the last forty-some years, because life is changing, technologies are changing or societal viewpoints are changing. These particular and some other not mentioned human developments have always been in flux and will continue to do so.

What astonishes me is the fact that whole layers of the modern Western Society are running around to "find" themselves. How is that? Well, what has made these layers of people the *Me now* Society? That generation came from the people that survived the last World War. Their fathers and mothers wanted their children not ever to live, as they had to endure. "Learn, become somebody, the world can be yours." The schools' rules were changed. Arrangements were made to get more people to go to school. The curricula were changed. Important subjects were dropped or watered down. Dr. Benjamin Spock was heralded as the overseer of raising American children. The schools started to teach what is right from wrong, not the family. The higher educational institutions started to teach "social-awareness," "social justice" and "fairness" doctrines. The teaching subjects of Geography and History were eliminated and combined into Social Studies.

The family structure started to change dramatically. Why so? Mother and father said: All of us have to have a better life. There are now more "things" available to us. All we need is more money. How can that be done? Both mother and father go to work. Now what? We put the kids into "safe and educational" places. Family breakfast is gone, lunch is gone and family dinners are slowly but steadily disappearing. Why? Either mom or dad come home at different times, no more scheduled eating time. Hah, we have microwaves now, or worse, store-prepared sandwiches. How about Saturday family life? We have to go shopping! There is no time to do that during the week. Eating on the fly on that day. Then comes Sunday. Let's go to church and show all that we are very successful. On the way home we stop at a place to eat. Ah, dad has to cut the grass, no time until that day. Dad will then do a great barbeque for Sunday dinner.

Elected officials and the courts make changes that should be good for the "common good." Sport games are way too competitive. Boys and girls should be treated as equals. All religions and beliefs should be diversified. Do not offend anyone; even if it is only one person that is offended. Oh yes and family structures are old fashioned. Father and mother figures are not important to raise a family. The village will raise the family. Politeness, courtesies and "moral" rights and wrongs no longer are observed or practiced. "I must have it all now, I deserve it" seems to be the mantra for many people.

Moral guideline? Ah, that is so old fashioned. Personal discipline? Why, I do what I want to do. There used to be rules established either by communities or by lawful authorities. Now look what is happening every day. People cross the streets at any time and any place. Some even do not look, as they diagonally cross a street. People will park where they like.

Then come the "Entitlements." We hear: 45 million Americans are on food stamps. Does anybody ask why that is so and who is getting these benefits? No. We hear: The corporations are making huge profits and the "workers" get nothing of the profits. Well, no corporations, no jobs. As for profits, companies always made profits. That is the whole idea behind that. Good profits, good jobs and possible extensions by the companies, therefore more jobs. This has worked well, so far. Tax breaks for all immigrants. Why? Millions of immigrants came to this country, including Herwig and Heidi, receiving nothing from any State! Most of us made it. Fair? Tough? You bet it was and it should be that way. Medical help for all people. How can that be done, except by raising taxes.

And now these "elected" politicians are saying that the Social Security and Medicaid payments are entitlements? Are they nuts? The "bad" corporations are paying into the system and so are the workers. And then we, in retirement, still pay taxes on these monthly payments!

Now I am hearing this: How come older Americans have more money than younger Americans? Hello! Who has worked for 50-60 years?

We are living in open class warfare. You do not believe that? Let me tell you. I still hear loud and clear the slogans of communism. Down with capitalism, long live the working classes and the farmers. Equal rights to all people, etc., etc. And then that ruling class trampled on the masses and ruined their economies to the point of total collapse. At the same time, these ruling people lived in luxurious style, far from the masses.

How about courtesies or being polite? Young people barge right in front of elders to enter doors. No more "Please" or "Thank you." Letters and packages are ignored. Telephones no longer exist. People are totally in the ether world of music and texting. The spoken and written language is being destroyed. Books are no longer read; people read "condensed" (I call it censored) versions or clips. The "news" over the airwaves is centralized and come in very short blurbs.

The political parties no longer represent the people. To get power is all there is now. Truth gets twisted to fit an agenda. Lies are being presented as facts and the population swallows it all, without ever challenging it. The politicians get reelected, the professors in colleges and universities have permanent positions and also get time off to do research without losing their jobs, but a soldier coming home from 2-3 assignments cannot find a job.

What happened in the 1960s and 1970s laid the groundwork for all the troubles we have now. Questions are being asked now what is going on. Why are we here in this condition? It must be somebody's fault. Well, the fault lies right in front of the people that are asking the questions. Of course they can't see that because they were not raised in families and educated in schools that would make them see these things, let alone have an answer to them.

Young people get deep into debt and then can't pay back the debt. That is stealing. They took the loans knowing what they were doing. It is nobody's fault but their own. How about professional and school sports? Wow is that a deep dish of trouble. The "salaries" of participants in various sport venues are way out of line when compared with the general population's incomes. For instance: $50 million for 5 years! School "athletics" have gone crazy. High school, college and university sports have become hallmarks feverishly supported by the media and the masses. The expenses involved are phenomenal! Are they not forgetting something? For instance, *learning.*

Why has the cost of higher education risen so sharply in the last 12-15 years? Who does that? Not the government and not the banks. It is done right at the schools. Nobody sees that?

It is my fervent hope and wish that people throughout our country would return to the realities of life presenting all of us with positive or negative events, no matter who we are. We as free people are responsible for our own actions, but, at the same time, should be able to express our own view. It is a right, as guaranteed as Freedom of Speech, in our Constitution.

I still maintain very good contacts with former professional associates or business contacts, most of us now in retirement. The work I did for mapmaking in the U.S.A. is still with me. Outside the fact, that I helped create or built up a number of American cartographic facilities over the years of my career, I was able to contribute in other ways to the general professional appearance of American mapping. I have known the people of The National Park Service Design Center in Harpers Ferry for many years. The NPS Design Center was one of my main accounts at R.R. Donnelley Mapping Division. Together we developed the mapping program for the entire NPS in the United States.

One of their very talented designers became a nationally known terrain artist using a computer to do graphic designs. Very soon we all learned that he became very proficient at it. The Government sent him to training sessions in Europe to sharpen his skills. He became very intrigued in the techniques of mapping terrain art and he and I spent a lot of time together talking about it. He started to attend major conferences and symposiums on the subject and the next thing he became involved with was the terrain art created by Heinrich C. Berran of Austria. The Chief of the Design Center, Vincent Gleason and I were instrumental in getting Heinrich Berran to come to the U.S. and paint four major mountain panoramas: The Cascades, Yellowstone and the Tetons, Yosemite and Denali. It was my fortune to spend a lot of time with Berran in the American West and also to visit him at his studio in Austria to look at the progress of the works, at the time of their creation.

After Berran's death, the NPS designer wrote a major article about Berran's work, using a lot of my input, consisting of material I had collected over the years based on my relationship and friendship with Heinrich Berran. He developed ShadedReliefArchive.com; a national archive of geographic map artwork. Among the works he collected and archived digitally are all the pieces of artwork commissioned by me to various artists in the

U.S. that I was able to rescue from going into a dump. The originals are now at the Library of Congress, in the Geography and Map Division. Within these works are some of the artwork I had created myself and a few are still in my possession and at one time, after my death, shall find their home also at the LOC. Mike and Peter shall take care of that.

I made these donations in June and July 2010, including a complete collection of R.R. Donnelley & Sons Company created road maps. In September 2014 I donated a collection of cartographic tools and implements. Over the decades Heidi and I had assembled quite a collection of these things and I had also received more of it when the rest of the cartographic companies here in Lancaster went out of business. The Library of Congress expressed an interest in that material so I catalogued it all and turned it over to the Library.

Screech—Stop My Life!
2011, 2012, 2013

A very unexpected event took place in my life and with that in Heidi's life. Cancer was discovered in my body!

About five years earlier I had developed psoriatic arthritis, a form of rheumatoid arthritis. It manifested itself in my toes and fingers and arm joints in a very painful way. First I received steroid shots and later was put on "mild" dosages of steroids taken orally. The pain in my toes disappeared, but became worse in my fingers, hands, arm joints and hip and knee joints. For about four years the doctors tried all sorts of medications on me, including some cancer medications that were supposed to help the arthritis.

I started to get "acid reflux" and medications were given to me to relieve that problem. Then I started to have difficulties when swallowing food. Heidi became worried and she got me to a gastroenterologist. After some serious tests, they announced to me on December 15, 2011, that I had esophageal cancer located on the bottom of the esophagus, at the entrance to the stomach. Merry Christmas. What happened next to me I do not wish upon anyone.

I have tried to write about my experiences concerning the various treatments and their results. So far, I am finding that too difficult a task. The memories are way too vivid and mentally really painful. Heidi has kept a complete diary concerning my daily activities and her personal reactions and feelings. In short, I went the "whole nine yards" of cancer treatments. I had radiation, chemotherapy and major surgery over the course of six months. A few times I came very close to losing my life because of serious reactions that I had to either medications, radiations or associated reactions to these. After that started the recovery. Now, one year after (this is July 2013), I am cancer free, although we go through all sorts of tribulations each time another CAT Scan needs to be taken. I am told that I have to overcome two years of cancer-free life, to have a decent chance of survival.

I most certainly have to thank Heidi a lot for her care of me during all these horrible months. She gave me mental and physical comfort, but very importantly, she made my body whole. The months of tube feeding were some of my roughest times and the stuff they prescribed was downright awful to digest. On top of that, its main ingredient was corn syrup!

Heidi would administer minerals and vitamins right through the tube into me! Thank you Heidi.

I am working on it! Thanks to Heidi's persistent watching of my food intake and the fact that I took up swimming again, I am doing fine under the circumstances. I want to live and enjoy doing just that. Heidi gave up swim working—to spend more time with me—so we are doing all we can to do fun things together. This year we have been in Florida already and we are planning to be in Maine with friends in August. We have booked a cruise to the Western Caribbean in November. God, I am thankful!

Epilogue

Every story should have, at the end, some final comments by the author. There will be no exception to this un-written rule by this writer.

This is being written toward the end of the year 2019, as Heidi and I are now living in the Brethren Village Retirement Community in Lititz, PA. Our relatives, and especially our friends, had asked me for a long time to write my life story. The process started about 18 years ago and the work is finished as best as I can make it, considering that the English language is not my first language. It amazes me with wonder and awe, that I was able to finish the story of my life. Eight years ago, it had looked like an impossible task, I am very grateful for my long life. If at times I sound somewhat opinionated or too set in my thinking, forgive me, this is the way I am. It is not done to hurt anybody's feelings, but, at this stage of my life, allow me the freedom to express my own mind and thoughts.

It is my sincere hope that I have somewhat succeeded in this endeavor, and in addition, I have also done all this to satisfy any curiosity a future generation might have on the subject of life in the last half of the 20th century.

Writing down my thoughts has always been one of my traits. I have filled folders by now with my reactions to travel impressions, political controversies, philosophical thoughts or my thinking about world religions. And always, most of it is influenced by my love for the Earth Sciences.

Throughout my life I have read quite a lot, especially anything connected with history and exploration. One thing that struck me and convinced me even more to write, is the fact that quite a bit of our knowledge of history is based on letters—letters that had been written centuries ago—letters of world leaders, politicians, soldiers in the trenches during the fight in horrendous wars or by ordinary people describing their love for one another or the land they are living in. Please people, start writing again, it will help future generations to understand what is was you tried to accomplish.